REVIEWS *of UNSTOPPABLE* (2014)

"Mr. Nader has set out on a formidable mission here— nothing less than bringing corporations and government back under effective control of their constituents, and doing so with trans-political and ideological alliances. In effect, he proposes to transform entrenched contemporary politics."

—The *Washington Times*

"In *Unstoppable*, Ralph Nader argues that there are in fact surprising areas of convergence between the left and the right . . . These are profound observations . . . Mr. Nader rails so effectively."

—The *Wall Street Journal*

ALSO BY RALPH NADER

Return to Sender: Unanswered Letters to the President, 2001–2015

Unstoppable

Told You So: The Big Book of Weekly Columns

Getting Steamed to Overcome Corporatism

The Seventeen Solutions: Bold Ideas for Our American Future

"Only the Super-Rich Can Save Us!"

The Seventeen Traditions: Lessons from an American Childhood

The Good Fight: Declare Your Independence and Close the Democracy Gap

In Pursuit of Justice: Collected Writings 2000–2003

The Ralph Nader Reader

Crashing the Party: Taking on the Corporate Government in an Age of Surrender

Canada Firsts

Unsafe at Any Speed: The Designed-In Dangers of the American Automobile

BREAKING THROUGH POWER

It's Easier than You Think

Ralph Nader

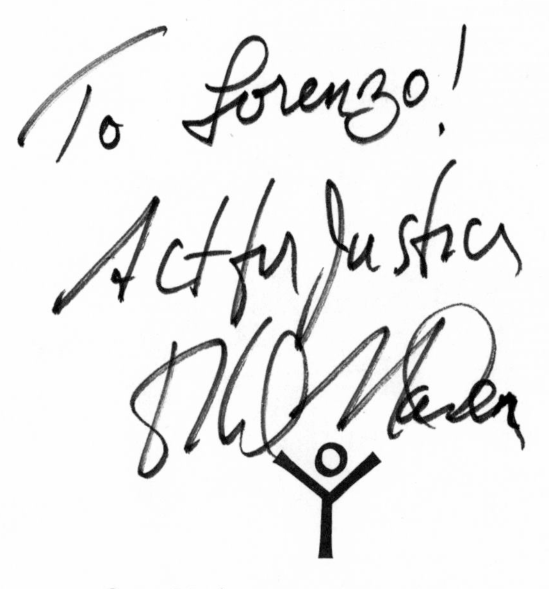

Open Media Series | City Lights Books

Open Media Series Editor: Greg Ruggiero

Library of Congress Cataloging-in-Publication Data
Names: Nader, Ralph, author.
Title: Breaking through power : it's easier than we think / Ralph Nader.
Description: San Francisco : City Lights Publishers, 2016. | Series: City lights open media
Identifiers: LCCN 2016008227 | ISBN 9780872867055 (paperback)
Subjects: LCSH: Democracy—United States. | Communities—United States. |
Power (Social sciences)—United States. | Wealth—United States. | Social justice—United States. | BISAC: POLITICAL SCIENCE / Economic Conditions.
| POLITICAL SCIENCE / Political Ideologies / Democracy. | POLITICAL
SCIENCE / Civics & Citizenship. | POLITICAL SCIENCE / Public Policy /
Economic Policy.
Classification: LCC JC423 .N245 2016 | DDC 322.40973—dc23
LC record available at https://lccn.loc.gov/2016008227

City Lights Books are published at the City Lights Bookstore
261 Columbus Avenue, San Francisco, CA 94133
www.citylights.com

To all citizens who wish to better the world and are seriously willing to dedicate some of their time, talent and resources to advance important causes.

I wish to acknowledge the sagacious assistance of Dr. Claire Nader and especially the dedicated attention to overall substantive details of my responsive editor, Greg Ruggiero, who proposed the book's approach.

I am also grateful to John Richard and his associates, Hunter Jones and Frank Garvey, for factchecking and proofreading.

—Ralph Nader

CONTENTS

ONE

PLUTOCRACY OF MAXIMUMS, DEMOCRACY OF MINIMUMS

When I was a student at Princeton University I learned from my anthropology studies that the concentration of power in the hands of the few is common to all cultures, societies, nations, tribes, cities, towns, and villages. Even where the thirst for self-governance and democracy is strong, as was the case in New England towns before the American Revolution against King George III, wealthy Tories were there too. In Central and Western Massachusetts, the farmers used the term "the River Gods" to describe the rich merchants using the Connecticut River as a profitable trading route. These days, most people protesting for economic justice use the term "the One Percent" to describe the ultra-small group of people who wield enormous influence over our society today.

There is something about the differences in skill, determination, lineage, avarice, and pure luck that stratifies most people from the rulers who dominate them. In the political realm, the few become dominant because they hoard wealth and are driven to exercise power over others. When a small group of people rules a society the political system is considered an oligarchy; when only money and wealth determine how a society is controlled, the political system is a plutocracy. From the standpoint of a democratic society, both oligarchy and plutocracy are inherently unjust and corrupt.

Of course there are variations in the degrees of authoritarianism and cruelty that each system exercises over the communities it relies upon for workers and wealth. Scholars have resorted to using phrases like "benign dictatorships" or "wise rulers" or "paternalistic hierarchies—" to describe lighter touches by those few who impose their rule over the many. Thomas Paine simply called them tyrannies. People, families, and communities can only take so much abuse before they rise up to resist. The job of the rulers is always to find that line and provide the lowest level of pay, security, housing, consumer protection, healthcare, and political access for society so that they can extract and hoard the greatest amount of wealth, power, and immunity from justice for themselves. In many ways, the majority of Americans live in a democracy of minimums, while the privileged few enjoy a plutocracy of maximums.

This small volume is not just about the ravages of power or the assaults against disadvantaged and downtrodden communities. The subject here is the dominating influence of the One Percent in business, politics, health, education, and society as a whole. Over the past fifty years, Americans have suffered the relentless commercialization of everyday life—their privacy and their childhoods, their parks and prisons, their public budgets and foreign policy, their schools and religious institutions, their elections and governments, and the most basic societal institution of them all: the family.

Consider all the family functions that have been outsourced to business. Eating, cleaning, childcare, counseling, therapy, entertainment, sports, lawn work, simple repairs, have been increasingly commercialized, commodified, packaged, and marketed back to us as products of luxury and convenience. Even mother's breast milk has been displaced by infant formula.

In a plutocracy, commercialism dominates far beyond the realm of economics and business; *everything is for sale*, and money is power. But in an authentic democracy, there must be commercial-free zones where the power of human rights, citizenship, community, equality, and justice are free from the corrupting influence of money. Our elections and our governments should be such commercial-free zones; our environment, air, and water should never fall under the control of corporations or private owners. Children should not be programmed by a huckstering economy where their vulnerable consciousness becomes the target of relentless corporate marketing and advertising.

American history demonstrates that whenever commerce dominates all aspects of national life, a host of ills and atrocities have not just festered and spread, but become normal—enslavement, land grabs, war, ethnic cleansing, serfdom, child labor, abusive working conditions, corrupt political systems, environmental contamination, and immunity from the law for the privileged few. History also shows that whenever there have been periods when enough of the country organizes and resists, we see movements of people and communities breaking through power. Progress is made. Rights are won. Education and literacy increase. Oppression is diminished. It was in this manner that people of conscience abolished the living nightmare imposed by the laws and whips of white enslavers. The nation moved closer to promises of "Life, Liberty, and the Pursuit of Happiness" expressed in the Declaration of Independence. We won more control over our work, our food, our land, our air, and our water. Women secured the right to vote. Civil rights were elevated and enforced. Public schools, improved environments, workplace collective bargaining, and consumer protections did not spontaneously evolve; they were won by people demanding them and breaking through power.

These moments of great progress are expressed in terms of new legislation, regulations, and judicial decisions that directly benefit the life, liberties, and pursuit of happiness of most Americans. From the abolition of slavery to the introduction of seat belts, great social gains have been achieved when people mobilize, organize, and resist the power of the few. The problem is that these liberating periods of humanitarian and civilizational progress are of shorter duration than the relentless commercial counterforces that discourage and disrupt social movements and their networks of support. Some commentators have used the bizarre term "justice fatigue" to describe the pullback that often occurs when communities of resistance are faced with increased surveillance, infiltration, harassment, and arrest. A more accurate term is repression.

My sister, Laura Nader, Professor of Anthropology at the University of California, Berkeley, encourages her students to study and compare how other cultures develop and improve their collective "common good." An illuminating comparison on a giant scale, for example, could be made between how the United States and our European allies and enemies developed after World War II. Maybe the difference in directions came from the complacency of the American victors, flush with "full employment" after a severe economic depression, in contrast to the motivation of Europe's surviving middle class, to return to a better life. In any event, a destitute France, Belgium, Holland, Germany, Italy, and Austria and the damaged Britain and Scandinavian nations took their traditions of strong labor unions, multi-party systems, and large co-ops to a level of productive social democracy that continues to shame the corporate-dominated, two-party tyranny that passes itself off for democracy in the United States.

Granted, these war-weary countries had their own plutocracies, their own One Percent, but those ruling elites were successfully kept in check by the rest of society, not the other way around as is the case today in the United States. This combination of factors, coupled with a hungry, impoverished population thirsting for a decent livelihood, raised the critical expectation level that drove the momentum for far-reaching social progress. In this manner, people in most Western European nations granted themselves important accommodations such as affordable universal healthcare, tuition-free higher education, bountiful private pensions, powerful job-protection laws, four weeks or more paid vacations, accommodating public transit, paid family sick leave, paid maternity leave, and free child care. People in the United States today, with the exception of some of those protected by labor unions, have permitted the wealthy class to deny them these benefits, allowing their taxes for example, to be spent on what is, by far, the world's biggest military budget and an ultra-invasive national surveillance system that allows the government to violate their privacy. People in Europe insist that their taxes be spent to enrich the health, education and well-being of the entire population, not just those with extreme wealth, so there is less grumbling. Some European communities even calibrate fines and fees based on income. People in Finland, for example, charge fines according to income level so that the financial sting is experienced more equally. As a result, a wealthy Finnish businessman recently found himself with a speeding ticket in the amount of about $58,000 (54,024 euros) "for traveling a modest, if illegal, 64 miles per hour in a 50 m.p.h. zone."[1]

Our country, which brags constantly about being number one in just about everything, managed to tie itself into knots after World War II. In 1947, a Republican Congress passed the notorious Taft-Hartley Act that handcuffed workers from forming new labor unions or expanding the ones that already existed. In 1948 the two-party duopoly smeared and suppressed the pro-labor efforts by the Progressive Party and its presidential candidate, former Vice President (under Franklin Delano Roosevelt) Henry Wallace. This was followed by more onerous restrictions on state ballot access and exclusions of third parties, enacted by both the Republicans and Democrats, that further stunted competitive choices of candidates and agendas. Today both parties increasingly represent the interests of big money, not the interests of the people, for it is big money that bankrolls their multi-million dollar election campaigns.

Almost as quickly as they emerged, radio and television stations in the United States conglomerated into big businesses beholden to the money and influence of their advertisers. While the Europeans devoted their post-war budgets to expanding public works, improving public facilities, social services, parks, and the arts, the United States squeezed civilian resources and channeled them into military budgets that drove the Cold War. It was not for nothing that President Eisenhower's farewell speech in 1961 is remembered most for warning about the many damaging effects, on both the economy and our freedom, of a burgeoning "military-industrial complex." His original draft contained the phrase "military-industrial-congressional complex" which was edited down to avoid alienating the members of Congress who could have actually done something to confront this deepening omnivorous crisis.

Concentrated power in the hands of the few really should matter to you. It matters to you if you are denied full-time gainful employment or paid poverty wages and there are no unions to defend your interests. It matters to you if you're denied affordable health care. It matters to you if you're gouged by the drug industry and your medication is outrageously expensive. It matters to you if it takes a long time to get to and from work due to lack of good public transit or packed highways. It matters to you if you and your children live in impoverished areas and have to breath dirtier air and drink polluted water and live in housing that is neglected by your landlord. It matters to you if your children are receiving a substandard education in understaffed schools where they are being taught to obey rather than to question, think and imagine, especially in regards to the nature of power.

If you're a little better off, it matters to you when your home is unfairly threatened with foreclosure. It matters to you when the nation is economically destabilized due to Wall Street's crimes, and your retirement account evaporates overnight. It matters to you if you can't pay off your large student loans, or if you can't get out from under crushing credit-card debt or enormous medical bills due to being under-insured. It matters to you if you are constantly worried about the security of your job, or the costly care of your children and elderly parents.

Increasing numbers of people in this country are living in a precarious and diminished democracy of minimums because we have collectively enabled the wealthy few to create for themselves a plutocracy of maximums. According to Oxfam, "runaway inequality has created a world where 62 people own as much as the poorest half of the world's population."[2] Oxfam advocates cracking down on tax dodging, and promotes increasing investment in public services and increasing the income of the lowest-paid workers in our society as important first steps in addressing the shameful disparity in wealth.

How many tens of millions of Americans live oppressed by an inadequate minimum wage, minimum housing security, minimum healthcare, minimum access to quality education, minimum access to participation in the political process or use of our courts, minimal access to quality air, food and water, and minimum protection from abuse by corporations? How much more should we take before we start refusing to live this way, with our rights, security, and well-being taken away by the One Percent and often marketed back to us as luxuries we cannot afford?

Back in the Great Depression, the brilliant British

economist John Maynard Keynes wrote that modern societies were reaching levels of production that would allow for solving what he called "the economic problem" of impoverishment. Since 1900, American productivity per capita has increased twenty-fold, adjusted for inflation. Why then is one in six people in the United States seriously impoverished, and why are nearly half of those employed the working poor? The general answer is because "the power of the plutocracy" impoverishes them. Most material gains and resources are diverted away from benefitting society as a whole and are hoarded to advantage the economic growth of the few, or diverted into counter-productive activities such as war, overloaded prisons, surveillance, wasteful promotions, and commercialization of all aspects of our lives.

In the 1950s, at Harvard Law School, the faculty purported to teach us "the law." We did not spend much time on the "lawlessness" of the rich and powerful (there wasn't even a single course or seminar on corporate crime), nor on how the powerful always intricately wrote and passed laws (containing legal loopholes, tax escapes, or corporate subsidies) that became predatory instruments against the general public. More broadly, we, the future leaders of the legal profession, lacked strenuous instruction about how those with raw power overwhelm the law, not just once in a while, but often enough to warrant calling this domination "power-law"—the twisted law of those in command of the powerful industries, their lobbying associations, and the corporate attorneys who prey upon the people, families, and communities that compose this nation. The effect has been—and continues to be—that, as Catherine Rampell recently wrote in the *New York Times*, "wealth has become more concentrated, in the hands (and bank accounts and houses) of the richest Americans."[3] Put more simply, the rich get richer while the rest of the country suffers.

By now, you might be wondering why in the world most seasoned law professors ignore such obvious realities. They must know that powerlaw is not restricted to lawlessness by police, the criminal courts, and the prisons. Many of my teachers had spent time working as government attorneys at regulatory agencies or the Justice Department, in addition to working with corporate law firms shaping and immunizing powerlaws for their lucrative corporate clients and business executives. What's going on here? Well, law schools are not driven by kindness or the common good; they are driven by the market and its pursuit of profit. Their curricula, with exceptions, focus on training most law students for lucrative corporate law practice. True, there are wonderful law school-based clinics charitably serving impoverished communities, but after graduation, debt-burdened law graduates mostly head for commercial practices. There they apply powerlaw and power-procedures against whatever rivals or adversaries their wealthy clients hire them to over-run. Citizens and communities underestimate the creative power of the corporate law firms who shun publicity as they irresponsibly protect the extreme misbehavior of the ultra-rich who hire them. The power of these ultra-rich, their attorneys, their media, and the influence their money buys constitute the core of plutocracy in the United States today.

Perpetual plutocracy-serving economic growth and the hoarding of wealth and power are not easy tasks in societies that claim to be democracies. Once in operation, political systems that become plutocracies come to view the power of citizens, communities, and the public interest mission of democracy itself as potential threats. Even when you're not consciously standing up to them, you are—collectively and individually—their adversaries. People running companies aim for their kind of endless economic growth by getting you to sign on the dotted line, click on "I Agree," succumb to their marketing ploys, and buy into their vapid commercial culture. They also invest heavily in obstructing you from using your full power as citizens armed with rights, privileges, and resources available to keep them, and others with authority, in check. For big corporations like Walmart, McDonald's, and Target, the big banks, credit card companies, and insurance companies, this penchant for control has worked to their advantage, assuming no one makes waves from outside their ring of domination. Thus power has concentrated in both Western Europe and the United States, but it has also been responsive to the organized interests of the people in dramatically different ways.

But what happens when people use their civil rights to demand more from the system? What happens, for example, when people peacefully picket in front of their places of work, on their lunch hour, for a higher minimum wage? What happens when other workers from other places show up too in order to express solidarity and defend those on the picket line from retaliation? What happens if these demonstrations become more frequent, and begin occurring in front of giant retail chains and involve an ever-increasing number of people? What happens if this begins to catch the attention of the local and national media, and the cause of the people picketing resonates with the conscience of the larger community? This is what happens: newspapers and other media start reporting the economic evidence and arguments of some think tanks and advocacy groups for a $12 or $15 minimum wage per hour, over three years, pulling up the minimum wage in companies where the CEO makes $11,000 per hour plus ample benefits.

Spread this activity out over two years and suddenly the minimum wage for thirty million workers, making less today than workers made way back in 1968, adjusted for inflation, becomes front-burner news and a front-line issue in local, state, and federal elections. This is what has been happening in the United States over the past few years. As a result, cities and states have started passing higher minimum wage laws, including referenda in four "red states" during the November 2014 elections. Those who stood up, who spoke out, who organized are amazed. And they should be. With fewer people than the population of New Britain, Connecticut (73,000), scattered around the country, demonstrating for a few hours, giving interviews to reporters or writing letters to newspapers and elected representatives, these people demonstrate that the wealthy people who run corporations do not win all the time. Breaking through power is easier than you think.

Pressured also by a few full-time citizen advocacy centers, the big companies are starting to announce higher wages and some better benefits. Too little, you rightfully say, and very late; still, it's a work in progress. But look at what a tiny number of hours and persons achieved with a little crucial help from largely one union—the Service Employees International Union. These workers and their champions possess a moral authority that resonated with many millions of disadvantaged families and their empathetic friends and relatives. Majorities in polls supported their cause.

These working people are beginning to prevail over management and their executive bosses because they were undeterred when people told them: "You can't win. You can't fight Walmart. The politicians are in the Big Boys' pockets." They broke through because they got others involved and because they put into practice what the great abolitionist Frederick Douglass meant when he declared: "Power concedes nothing without a demand."

In addition to stimulating the economy, creating more jobs, and establishing less need for public welfare assistance, the movement for a better living wage presents a useful lesson. It teaches how little it often takes to change the balance of power between the dominating and the dominated, especially when there is overwhelming public opinion supporting those fighting for their long over-due rights. These lessons can, and should, be applied to winning the myriad of public interest, ecological, and civil rights struggles that the ultra-rich and their commercial interests obstruct: some of these include increasing wages for working people, decreasing militarism and crushing levels of military spending, providing decent and affordable housing and healthcare, reducing corporate carbon emissions in order to prevent catastrophic climate change, strengthening diversity, and enabling democracy at all levels.

"We live in a beautiful country," writes historian Howard Zinn. "But people who have no respect for human life, freedom, or justice have taken it over. It is now up to all of us to take it back."[4] To better assess what it specifically takes to do just that, it is important to understand how the people profiting from plutocratic forces strategically and regularly dominate old and new circumstances with powerful controlling processes.

TWO

TO ORGANIZE IS TO INITIATE RESISTANCE AND CHANGE

In the 1920s, near the end of his spectacular career as our country's most prominent fighter for working people, labor leader, presidential candidate, orator, and all-around progressive Eugene Debs was asked by a reporter: "Mr. Debs, what do you regret the most in your lifelong struggle for justice?"

Debs looked at him and replied: "What do I regret the most? I regret that the American people can have almost anything they want under our Constitution, but they seem not to want much of anything at all."

An indefatigable exhorter, Debs may be excused for feeling exhausted after so many decades of trying to raise the expectations of working families. Woodrow Wilson made sure he was jailed for simply speaking out against the nation's entry into World War I. Debs knew what war does to societies. The very avoidable "Great War" broke the momentum of our nation's rising progressive reform movement, ushered in the era of red-baiting, and directly set the stage for World War II. Most crucially, the aggressive expansion of the American Empire and military state distracted and lowered the expectation levels for American democracy and civic society. Debs knew full well how power structures thwarted the general population's expectations for the good life and paved the way for entrenched austerity and misery, despite a growing gross domestic product.

Hope and positive expectations provide some of the most basic motivation for attempting to improve the human condition. Once people are inspired, and hope and expectations for change are aroused, the power of democracy voices a "rumble from the people." Plutocrats were aghast when President Richard Nixon, responding to the rumble of the 1960s, signed into law the basic environmental, consumer and worker safety regulatory frameworks that are still in force to this day, along with the legislation establishing the Occupational Safety & Health Administration, the Environmental Protection Agency, and the Consumer Product Safety Commission. To be sure, the rumble from the people also drove some pretty good legislators to Congress and jolted incumbents—mostly Democrats—into heeding some of the popular will.

Even though Nixon was a red-baiting Republican, he was also paranoid about "liberals." He responded to public pressure, and even went beyond the Congress that rejected his proposals for a minimum-income policy, a drug bill that emphasized rehabilitation over incarceration, a better health insurance plan than President Clinton later introduced, and Congressional voting rights for the residents of the District of Columbia.

Actively engaged in Washington at that time, I watched Nixon's political antennae quiver and turn again and again, ending with his ultimate betrayal of right-wingers in 1973 when he instituted wage and price controls to fight inflation. Nixon went against the grain of the plutocracy of his time because he feared social unrest and felt that the national change in political climate warranted, for him at least, "extreme expediency." He sometimes responded to the rumble.

The U.S. plutocracy and general population reacted very differently toward Nixon's performance. While many in America collectively seemed not to see how a little rumble could result in material and political advancement of their well-being and as a result did not fight for further progress, the stung corporatist class saw all too clearly what was possible. They knew democracy could regulate their profiteering, so they greatly remobilized their forces to subordinate and minimize institutions, organizations, networks, and individuals dedicated to expanding democracy.

In August 1971, Lewis Powell, a corporate lawyer in Richmond, Virginia, and soon-to-be Justice of the U.S. Supreme Court, issued what would later be referred to as the "Powell memorandum." The memorandum offered his analysis of the power balance in Washington and pronounced it a crisis for big business. The forces of reform had brought many industries under a variety of regulations, and business was on the defensive. Powell urged a fundamental expansion and strengthening of the corporate lobbying apparatus, using some of the very techniques that the consumer, environmental, and other interests were deploying. These included corporate think tanks, aggressive use of the media, advancing business views on campus and in the curriculum, greater involvement in elections, and a mobilization of chief executives. It was time, Powell said, to mount an energetic far-reaching counterattack against those who, he believed, would subvert the free enterprise system.

The collision of the operational interests of private commerce and public governance has elicited warnings going back to Thomas Jefferson, Abraham Lincoln, and Teddy Roosevelt. The following quotes illustrate the historic concerns of our country's leaders about unbridled corporate power:

> "Big business is not dangerous because it is big, but because its bigness is an unwholesome inflation created by privileges and exemptions which it ought not to enjoy."
>
> —Woodrow Wilson

> "In the councils of government, we must guard against the acquisition of unwarranted influence, whether sought or unsought, by the military-industrial complex."
>
> —Dwight Eisenhower

> "The government has ceased to function, the corporations are the government."
>
> —Theodore Dreiser

> "The citizens of the United States must control the mighty commercial forces which they themselves called into being."
>
> —Theodore Roosevelt

President Franklin Delano Roosevelt sent legislation to Congress in 1938 to create a commission to investigate concentrated corporate power with a message that contained the prophetic warning that "ownership of government by a group, or by another controlling private power, is fascism."

Although fascism, on paper, is an antonym to democracy, during World War II, the atrocities of Hitler and Mussolini (whose PhD thesis was on the subject of the corporate state) revealed just how nightmarish fascism can be in practice. America's Founding Fathers wrote a Constitution that never once uses the words "corporation," "company," or "political parties." Their use of language reflected their antipathy toward the domineering influence of empire and big businesses in their communities and lives. To American Revolutionaries, companies with territorial monopolies such as the East India Company and Hudson's Bay Company were simply different faces of the tyrannical British Crown. Framers such as Jefferson and Madison viewed political parties contemptuously as "factions" of bickering self-interest. Jefferson puts it eloquently: "I hope that we shall crush in its birth the aristocracy of our monied corporations, which dare already to challenge our government to a trial of strength, and bid defiance to the laws of our country."

If "We the People" are the sole subjects of the U.S. Constitution, why is it that we are ruled by large corporations and their largely indentured servants—the Republican and Democratic Parties—who continually seek to narrow and control the political spectrum for voters? The easy answer is that "We the People" have allowed these plutocratic forces to slowly siphon away our power.

This dynamic is inadequately recognized when evaluating the need to expand civic responses, security, and defense of public sovereignty. Those with enormous wealth and private power are able to over-reach into and dominate in the public sphere because they are inherently sensitive to their surroundings and emerging challenges to their demand for constant concentrated growth. Before and after the American Revolution, there has been a continuing daily tension between contending private commercial pursuits and common civic values. The historical struggles to stop white people from enslaving blacks, to provide protections to workers and farmers, and to end child labor are illustrations of such tension.

Most major religions and spiritual philosophies going back thousands of years have warned their adherents not to give too much power to wealth. Their wisdom and traditions teach that the obsessive drive for gold, money, and profit is a formidable deviation from other more important spiritual practices that strive to center community on non-market values such as love, generosity, kindness, cooperation, and non-violence. In our own country, American Transcendentalist Henry David Thoreau made this point throughout his writings, especially in "Life Without Principle" where he says "the world is a place of business" and that "the ways by which you may get money almost without exception lead downward." Thoreau saw where the nation was and where it was going. He preferred jail to paying taxes while the United States was invading Mexico under false pretexts in order to take land at gunpoint.

Again and again the tension between commercial imperialism and an ethical life has played out dramatically in American history. With few exceptions, America's business leaders said **NO** to the idea of revolting against the British monarchy. During the Revolution, however, expedient merchants and manufacturers were willing to profit from selling weapons, food, and other supplies to the Continental Army. The commercialists often sided with the Tories, and the quality of the goods they sold to the Revolutionaries was often so defective or contaminated as to outrage General George Washington.

In later decades, commercialists, now armed with ever larger treasuries and shielded by the armor of corporate law, consistently said **NO** to efforts to end child labor, **NO** to starting labor unions, **NO** to the regulation of railroad and banking abuses, **NO** to the 40-hour week and progressive taxation, **NO** to antitrust laws and the regulatory agencies we take for granted such as the Food and Drug Administration or the Federal Trade Commission, **NO** to a woman's right to vote (they feared the women's vote against exploiting child labor and cheating consumers), and **NO** to the minimum wage, Social Security, universal healthcare, and to the latter-day drives to protect the environment, empower consumers, reduce government secrecy, protect ethical whistleblowers, and even to reduce commercial fraud on the government as with Medicare and military contracts.

Since the battle for auto safety in the 1960s, public interest groups, consumer protection organizations, and a diverse variety of social networks have worked relentlessly to break through the battalions of lobbyists and lawyers paid by corporate interests to strenuously say **NO** to what is safe, healthy, fair, and ecologically sustainable. Democracy-centered movements have forced many corporate titans to retreat, adjust and reset their business models to take the well-being of communities, families, individuals, and the environment into account. Unfortunately, most gains that have been won remain precarious victories under constant threat by the corporate forces that have the big budgets to influence policy with money. The average wage, inflation adjusted, peaked for a majority of people in 1973, and there has been no over-arching economic and regulatory legislation benefiting the general population since the mid-1970s. A high water mark attempt to establish a consumer protection watchdog agency was derailed by corporate pressure during the presidency of Jimmy Carter in 1978. The degree to which the plutocracy has dominated and defeated efforts to advance the public interest in the United States has steadily expanded over the last 40 years.

I was reminded of the depth and resilience of even small business organizations during a November 2014 visit to Joan and Calvin Clark Jr.'s Corvair Parts business in Massachusetts.[5] I had given a surprised Mr. Clark an advance call, and he and his wife and business partner graciously greeted me when I dropped by one late afternoon to see their operation. I was astonished when I surveyed the headquarters building and learned of the several large Quonset huts used to stock and sell commercial parts throughout the country and abroad. Many of the Clarks' customers are among the 6,500 dues-paying members of the Corvair Club of America, which is remarkably well-organized and even stages an annual national convention. (They invited me to speak to them in 1997. To break the ice I opened by saying we in this room should all agree that here are some of the best drivers in the world.)

The Clarks started with a love of cars, two personally-owned Corvairs, and a search for parts. Today they run a business with 28 full-time employees. The catalogs of Corvair-related parts and products that they market are each about one-inch thick! All of this for a car that General Motors stopped producing in 1969; it was disliked by its dealers and embroiled the company in scores of liability lawsuits.

Now compare the Clarks' bustling enterprise with the only two multi-staffed national auto safety advocacy groups in our country—the Center for Auto Safety and the Advocates for Highway and Auto Safety—both in Washington D.C. Together these advocacy groups have about twelve full-time staffers occupying approximately the same amount of floor space as one of the Clarks' Quonset huts. Besieged by auto industry lobbyists, they have to deal with millions of recallable vehicles, weak safety standards, controversial legislation, and lagging government regulations. I believe their combined annual non-profit budget is smaller than the Clarks' hard-earned annual revenues. Neither public interest group has any annual convention of members to discuss ways to reduce the sizable, but very much diminished (thanks to federal policies) casualty toll on the highways. Though their work has been very impressive and effective given their limited size, on occasion these two organizations have a difficult time meeting payroll.

On a much larger scale, the principles that drive large, profit-centered corporations are the antithesis of those that drive democracy-centered societies. Corporatists argue that in order to function most effectively, big business must manage workers' performance through a top-down command structure. They never use the word authoritarian to describe themselves, although they are very vertically autocratic; instead they cite the "free market" as their disciplinarian.

Let's examine large global corporate structures and their lack of external discipline. Exxon/Mobil, Pfizer, Citigroup, General Motors, Lockheed/Martin, Proctor & Gamble, United Health Care, Comcast/NBC Universal, Apple, and many other giants garner revenues as large as numerous nation states around the world. Most are global in operation, but there is no public global government holding them accountable to communities of people. Just the opposite; there are dictatorial trade agreements that corporatists conjure up in order to subordinate the general population's labor, consumer, and environmental protections—a stunning end run around our courts and legislatures. These protections are seen as "non-tariff trade barriers" to be subordinated to the priority of international commerce.

Apart from size and range, these global authoritarian entities have a clear and obsessive unity of purpose: money—money for bosses, money for shareholders, money to buy lawyers and politicians to take down laws and whatever else slows the pace of hoarding wealth. Over the decades there has been no debate raging inside Exxon or Peabody Coal about whether it is best to move to solar energy in place of the fossil fuels that are connected to toxic contamination and catastrophic climate change. To the contrary, Exxon has spent millions to mislead the public and delay, for as long as possible, the world from finding out that catastrophic climate change is directly linked to what makes them money: extracting and selling fossil fuels to be used in a way that contaminates and destabilizes Earth's biosphere.[6] Part of the misinformation campaign includes experts like Wei-Hock Soon, a scientist at the Harvard-Smithsonian Center for Astrophysics, and others who have influenced policy by countering the claims that the fossil fuel business is destroying the planet, while they quietly receive large sums of money from precisely those businesses.[7]

Merck and Eli Lilly aren't having internal battles over what is best for families in the United States; they are not investing in the study of whether or not the nation will be more secure if everyone has Medicare; they are not lobbying politicians in Washington, D.C. to save thousands of lives of men, women and children through more affordable healthcare and access to doctors and hospitals. Raytheon and General Dynamics do not worry about how many of their weapons are being purchased and used for crimes, massacres, and other atrocities. For decades McDonald's showed little anxiety or internal dissension about leading the spiral of disease-producing child obesity with its cardiac diet, while undermining parental authority. People at Coca-Cola have not worried about the long-term health consequences for children who consume the caffeine and sugar cocktail Coke markets all over Earth; instead Coca-Cola has spent lavishly on complex public relations efforts in attempt to divert attention away from the links between their products and childhood obesity and other diseases.[8] Nor did those calling the shots at Phillip Morris and R.J. Reynolds have any serious qualms about continuing to deceptively market and sell an addictive and lethal product after it was known to be the cause of a national cancer epidemic that, the U.S. Surgeon General estimated, destroys over 400,000 American lives annually. None of these or other global companies has much loyalty to country, community, or the fragile ecological stability upon which all life is dependent. "Corporate patriotism" are not two words that come together in people's minds.

The generations of businesspeople who enriched themselves from coal, lead, and asbestos corporations not only continued their business as usual in light of evidence that their activities caused widespread illness, but spent lavishly to derail life-saving laws and lawsuits while millions of people were contaminated, sickened, and killed from exposure. The death and damage caused by these and other similar industries has wrought staggering economic losses to families and to the nation in terms of taxpayer-funded remediation. Lead damaged the brains of very young, often poor, children, who, in their innocence, munched on flakes of lead-based paint, while toxic dust from coal mines blackened the lungs and snuffed the lives of hundreds of thousands of coal miners. I saw this slow-motion massacre firsthand in the hollows of Appalachia and later with sick coal miners I helped to bring to Congressional hearings that finally led to the Coal Mine Safety and Compensations laws in 1969. Decade after decade these three unregulated substances produced deadly silent violence and took a substantial toll, even though the people reaping profits from their sale knew of the lethal effects of these substances for decades. Change simply was not going to come until enough families, grieving from the preventable loss of their loved ones, finally broke through power and demanded that lawmakers enact bans on lead in gasoline and paint, the prohibition of most uses of asbestos, and the regulation of coal dust in underground mines.

Did any of these companies ever express remorse, regret or a public apology? Did any of their executives get forced out in disgrace or were any of these bosses prosecuted or jailed or personally subjected to civil fines? No. Could anybody stop victimized communities from at least demanding a public apology?

A recurrently devastating trait of the people who profit through large corporate entities is their insulation from decisive community sanctions and impunity from laws that send other less-endowed perpetrators to prison. Individuals who commit capital crimes risk being sentenced to capital punishment. Corporations and their bosses who enjoy the rights and privileges of the powerful simply do not bear the same risks as individuals who perpetrate similar crimes of predation or lethal neglect and abuse. Corporate personhood not only results in an impossibility of "equal justice under law" between living people, communities, and corporations; it coolly enforces how a plutocracy of maximums and democracy of minimums becomes normalized.

More deeply evasive is how corporate culture tolerates desecration of wildlife and nature, and normalizes how preventable violence is negligently—and often knowingly—inflicted on the people who they employ, who they market their products to, or who live in communities contaminated by the poisonous substances released from mining, manufacturing, or the shipping of lethal products. Traditionally, generally accepted accounting principles do not cover such imposed devastation and register such deficits against the assets of the corporations. Puckish economists would refer to this evasion as "externalizing the internalities" or, simply put, making the victims absorb the criminals' losses.

So deeply embedded are these corporate escapes from responsibility that street-crime casualties receive far, far greater attention from law enforcement, public budgets, mass media, and politicians running for elected office. The kinds of violence addressed or ignored grimly reflect the gross imbalance between raw power and public safety in any society. Compare communities of color to corporate society. How often do police accidentally shoot and kill bankers who are committing financial crimes, stealing homes, and plunging the nation into economic instability and recession? The nightmarish truth is difficult to absorb.

The above examples of corporate crime and violence are but a few of the myriad of cases of documented, preventable human and economic casualties. But they suffice to make the point that the people creating plutocracy through big corporations are very unlike you or me. Shorn of retribution or shame, they take more and more privileges and immunities for themselves while stripping our society of its capacity to deter and repel their damaging operations. The *Wall Street Journal* and the *New York Times*, among other mainstream publications, report repeatedly how people use corporations to lie, cheat, steal, and destroy lives.

Sometimes the name of a business gets so tarnished with criminal accusation that those invested in it deem it strategic to change its name. This was the case with those making money from the notorious Blackwater Corporation. The company came to wide notoriety after several of its mercenary employees were accused of perpetrating a massacre on September 16, 2007, in Nisour Square, Baghdad, in which 31 unarmed civilians were shot, 14 of whom died as a result of their wounds. Blackwater changed its name to Xe Services in 2009, then changed names again in 2011 to Academi. Four of Blackwater's mercenaries were found guilty and lightly sentenced in 2015.[9]

Over time, the public has demanded that boundaries be enforced around these rapacious entities to prevent them from minimizing non-commercial values, rights, institutions—democracy itself—into non-existence. Such boundaries are supposed to be implemented through mechanisms of regulations, courts, legislatures, elections and initiatives by organized stakeholders such as labor unions, housing advocates, consumer organizations, and environmental protection groups. But these defense and advocacy mechanisms for democracy-based community and the common good have been too static and vulnerable to the relentless assaults that corporations wage with enormous budgets, vast stables of lawyers, new technologies, and increasingly, capital flights to receptive jurisdictional sanctuaries abroad.

To observe the intricate predatory tactics of corporations is to see these brilliant "legal fictions" rampaging over society. Many of these forces require heavy deductible spending on attorneys, accountants, surveillance, security, and academic consultants. And media-savy public relations firms often give corporations license to maneuver deviously, and commit acts of espionage and infiltration against those who dare to investigate them or hold them accountable. "Many of the world's largest corporations and their trade associations," writes Gary Ruskin, "including the U.S. Chamber of Commerce, Walmart, Monsanto, Bank of America, Dow Chemical, Kraft, Coca-Cola, Chevron, Burger King, McDonald's, Shell, BP, BAE, Sasol, Brown & Williamson and E.ON—have been linked to espionage or planned espionage" against people and organizations who speak out against them, protest their practices, or conduct investigations into harm being committed in regards to environmental contamination, food safety, pesticides, nursing home practices, gun control, animal rights, and workers' rights.[10]

Taken all together, those being enriched are those who are advancing plutocracy over democracy, and they are bolstered by the modern, giant commercial corporation as a power-concentrating machine that seeks endless economic growth for itself by undermining, dominating, and diminishing the democratic spaces and regulatory institutions of national public interest, media, human services, and environment. To make it all sound less disastrous, they delicately call the process "privatization" and "deregulation." They do lose battles and skirmishes, as we have seen, but over the past two generations they have won wars resulting in low-wage, corporatized countries whose differing cultures have made little difference. Profits for the very few continue while the rest of the planet faces ecological destabilization, poverty, mass surveillance, and war.

Paradoxically, we are in a golden age of books, documentaries, and films that sharply expose the abuses, crimes and authoritarian essence of corporate commercialism. Never have so many of these muckraking gems been produced and never, with few exceptions, have they had less impact for change. Their minimal effect, aside from their small indie audiences, is mainly due to the strategically-planned takeovers of the very democratic institutions—from the public airwaves to Congress—that otherwise would have made it easier for these exposés to mobilize forces of public resistance.

Every March, there is a grand environmental film festival in Washington D.C. where expertly-produced narratives are shown about what is happening to contaminate, wreck, or render unusable the Earth's land, water, air, climate, food, and animal life. The audiences are diverse in age, ethnic, and racial composition but decidedly middle to upper income. The audiences are enthusiastic and inquiring. When the festival is over, so is any likelihood of dedicated action beyond what they brought to the auditorium. They are more informed, perhaps more discouraged, but no one pools their names for any post-film collective action. Hasn't that been the norm with such crowd-getters as *Fahrenheit 9/11* or *Sicko* by Michael Moore? They seem to only produce interesting memories, leaving mostly just footprints in the sand. That is what happens when an empire-minded plutocracy expands within a demoralized citizenry and neglected democracy.

Were Shakespeare around to write a play about our times, perhaps his opening line to the Plutocracy would be "Get thee to the Oligarchy. Blend yourselves together and thou shalt rule invincible forever after." For that is what is transpiring. But, as we shall see, such an influence of corporation upon state does not have to be either invincible or forever. Not when we understand the wondrous flexibility of corporate planning, should it choose, from time to time, to bend in order not to break.

For more than two centuries the chief obstacles to commercial hegemony over society have been the three branches of democratic government invested with authority to legitimately establish and use the force of law to protect the life, liberty, and pursuit of happiness of the general population and promote policies on behalf of the common good. Corporations understand that their weakness lies in the fact that people, at least on paper, still have the authority to use police power to counter corporate predation, coercion, and crime with enforcement of the law. It is for this reason that the core priority of commercial strategy has been to influence government at all levels. Simply put, the wealthy few invest heavily in shaping laws that strive to place unlimited private property and corporate expansion above and beyond all else, including the lives of people, the health of communities, protection of what we own in common, the capacity of society to function as a democracy, and the stability of the living biosphere itself.

The muscle that plutocracy deploys to control governments and the public sphere is anything but obscure. The wealthy few unleash a torrent of money (through PACs) into election campaigns and induce candidates to continually constrict and narrow the range of debate to those issues that serve corporate growth. The wealthy few donate lavishly to both parties and support their exclusionary tactics via state ballot barriers meant to prevent insurgent third parties and independents from reaching voters. They elaborately nurture incumbents by "wining, dining and golfing them," dangling the prospects of lucrative positions for them should they retire or be defeated in forthcoming elections. Not a bad package for selling your soul on behalf of merging the rich few with the political few. No one put it more crisply than Pennsylvania's Republican Senator, Boies Penrose, who told his business supporters over 110 years ago: "I believe in a division of labor. You send us to Congress, we pass laws under . . . which you make money . . . and out of your profits, you further contribute to our campaign funds to send us back again to pass more laws to enable you to make more money."

Fast forward to August 2015, when the *New York Times*, using Federal Election Commission reports and Internal Revenue Service records, concluded that "fewer than four hundred families are responsible for almost half the money raised in the 2016 Presidential Campaign, a concentration of political donors that is unprecedented in the modern era."[11] The Republican presidential candidates and their Super PACs have tapped into just 130 families and their businesses for over half the money raised, noted the *Times*.

Let's name names as does the *Times*. Hedge funder Robert Mercer poured 11 million dollars into the presidential run and Super PACs for Senator Ted Cruz. No problem, hedge funds are given an unconscionable tax break, criticized by Warren Buffett and others, that allows hedge funds to pay much lower capital gains taxes for this ordinary income.

Kelcy L. Warren, billionaire owner of a Texas-based energy company, poured six million dollars into Rick Perry's coffers in order to boost his presidential run. The tax subsidies for oil and gas are big, entrenched, and legendary.

Larry Ellison, one of the world's richest men and founder of Oracle Corporation, budgeted three million dollars for Senator Marco Rubio's campaigns (followed by billionaire investor Paul Singer's checkbook). Oracle has been receiving corporate welfare for years, including lavish research and development tax credits.

The husband-and-wife team of Farris Wilks and JoAnn Wilks has given five million dollars each—a mere sliver earned from the tax loopholes that their oil and gas fracking business has exploited over the years—to various presidential campaign vehicles set up for Senator Ted Cruz. Meanwhile, an assortment of tax avoiders placed a few million dollars on Jeb Bush, chump change, but it would be a mistake not to cover all the bases paving the way for more corporatist government. The cash register politics practiced by Senator Boies Penrose has never been more widespread than it is today. The Gilded Age that Penrose enjoyed has turned into the Platinum Age of today, while the gulf between rich and poor has deepened into a chasm.

The algorithms of control go deeper than just money and favors. Business strategists have long worried about the Democratic Party's occasional waywardness, particularly with President Franklin Roosevelt's New Deal. Democrats for a long while relied on labor union money as a mainstay, along with the more popular message of the Democrats being for "working families." In 1980, Congressman Tony Coehlo (D-CA) started moving the Democratic Party on the path to soliciting business campaign money, big time.

Almost immediately I could see the practical results for these paymasters: fewer Congressional hearings into corporate abuses, fewer regulatory actions for mandatory standards, and therefore, less mass-media coverage, less public indignation, further entrenchment of a democracy of minimums and a plutocracy of maximums.

The major commercial newspapers, magazines, and television networks are more likely to cover corporate shenanigans, especially given their bread-and-butter advertisements, if they view corporations as having significant adversaries in Congress. I learned this firsthand when I used to direct my letters exposing destructive behavior by big business to responsive senators such as the powerful chairman of the Senate Commerce Committee, Warren Magnuson (D-WA). Reporters on Capitol Hill knew that going to Magnuson was not tilting at windmills, given his sterling record of enacting pro-consumer and other reforms. When I couldn't locate influential sponsors on Capitol Hill, there was no media coverage, no matter how important the content was in regards to the people's well-being.

Still, the politicos of business went further. Their goal was to move into both major political parties to such a degree that the differences between them regarding their interests would pale before their fundamental similarities. The two parties even colluded and bankrolled, in 1987, the takeover of the presidential debates from the League of Women Voters through a private corporation that was given a name that sounds like an unbiased non-profit or government agency—the Commission on Presidential Debates. Fully exposed in George Farah's pioneering book, *No Debate*, this maneuver meant that an entity representing the narrow interests of the two political parties—not a non-partisan body open to the diverse political spectrum—would decide the rules regarding who would participate in the debates, how debates would be staged, right down to which reporters were to be invited to ask largely predictable questions before well-filtered audiences, conveyed to the voters by obedient television networks. The takeover inspired former *CBS News* anchor Walter Cronkite to publicly declare at Harvard University in 1991: "The debates are part of the unconscionable fraud that our political campaigns have become . . . the candidates participate only with the guarantee of a format that defies meaningful discourse."[12]

Not surprisingly, there was a rare stumble when the Commission allowed Ross Perot to participate in the widely-viewed debates in 1992, after which he got over nineteen million votes. After that, the Commission would never again permit anyone outside the two-wing business party to participate in the national debates. That exclusion has applied to major third-party presidential candidates, such as myself and Pat Buchanan, despite national polls showing huge sectors of the country wanting us included, if only as a cure against drowsiness. At that time, there was no other way to reach tens of millions of voters with such depth and immediacy. The radio, television, and major newspapers made sure of that blackout. My filling six major arenas across the country in 2000, including Madison Square Garden, did not reach two percent of the people that one televised presidential debate inclusion would have provided. Naturally, voters did not hear the debates address any of the changes that a majority of the nation's voters wanted, including full Medicare for all; living wages; prosecution of corporate crimes; cleaning up of elections; de-escalation of increasingly militarized and militant U.S. foreign policy; a public works program to repair the country's infrastructure; abolition of corporate subsidies, bailouts, and giveaways; augmentation of consumer, labor, and environmental protections and attacking specific corruption in Washington, D.C. My 2004 presidential campaign in 50 states never received more than a total of five minutes on the national TV network's evening news broadcasts that use our public airwaves.

As if these assaults against any semblance of a robust and politically diverse democracy were not enough, commercial interests did not object and often encouraged the gerrymandering of electoral districts, allowing state legislators to pick their voters. All the easier and cheaper to control matters when only one major party is in charge of state government. Without viable electoral variety and competition, there is no democracy by definition; there are only coronations, as Democrats have shown in Massachusetts and Republicans have shown in Texas. Many incumbents run entirely unopposed.

So how do the people enriched by companies and their sprawling trade associations, such as the U.S. Chamber of Commerce and hundreds of more specialized associations, keep the lawmakers in line on Capitol Hill? First, they keep the money and reminders flowing throughout the year. Washington is awash with targeted fundraising parties where the lobbyists can come and do the reminding with highly sought-after direct access to the legislators. Political action committee parties are about more than just money; they are valuable opportunities for private access to influence and guide the Solons and their staff.

Second, the business lobbying industry works on placing its people into high government positions at the cabinet and regulatory agency levels. Never worry that the Secretaries of Defense or the Secretaries of the Treasury are ever going to be nominated if their nominations are contrary to the wishes of the captains of the military-industrial complex or Wall Street's big bankers.

There is a Wall Street-to-Washington shuttle and a regular exchange between the large corporate law firms and high political appointments. For example, President Obama's former Attorney General, Eric Holder, came from the aggressive Washington law firm of Covington and Burling that worked on behalf of the tobacco, drug, oil, and banking industries. In June 2015 Holder resigned, and guess what? He returned to an even more lucrative partnership with Covington and Burling. He repeatedly refused to meet with civic groups or even consider their proposal to establish a crucial corporate crime database. This is a proposal long supported by House Judiciary Committee ranking member, Representative John Conyers, so that the Justice Department, with larger media interest, could better know about and plan a wider law enforcement drive against the rising waves of corporate crime. Small wonder that Holder did not prosecute the Wall Street crooks who destabilized the national economy in 2008–2009 while dropping their own derelict companies and exiting with abundant personal enrichments. Instead, the FBI, the Department of Homeland Security, and local police, acting as if democracy posed a criminal threat to plutocracy, often cracked down against the national movement of people that protested Wall Street, political corruption, and crimes of economic mass destruction.[13] More than 7,000 ordinary Americans who participated in the movement's activities were subjected to mass surveillance, mass arrests, and jail in the period between 2011 and 2012.[14]

The business lobbies can take a lion's share of the credit for the present two-party duopoly that ministers to their demands. Going for the same campaign dollars, the Republican and Democratic Parties have condoned the increasingly influential role of private money in public elections. They have allowed the tightening dominance of the military-industrial complex to continue without even demanding that the Pentagon's sprawling books be subject to annual audit. That's the equivalent of half of the entire federal government's discretionary expenditures without an annual audit year after year!

Taken as a whole, the two political parties have similar foreign and military policies that continue to ensnare the American empire into increasingly uncontrollable quagmires and blowbacks, such as the invasions, occupations, and sociocides of Iraq, Afghanistan, and Libya. Both political parties monetize elections and oppose greater electoral diversity and competition, and see no civil liberties and civil rights transgressions in that militant position. They have both supported the growth of the corporate welfare state, which helps explain why there is a left/right convergence among the people against such sprawling crony capitalism.

Differing rhetoric about corporate taxes has not led the Democrats to really make severing tax escapes for corporations a commitment with a program that they campaign on between and during elections. The Democrats have better rhetoric regarding protections for consumers, labor, and the environment, but it is remarkable how much *more* energetic the Republicans are in marshalling resources to get things done in the opposite direction. While the Democratic Party does more to defend Americans' safety net—Medicare, Medicaid, Social Security—it also protects Obamacare's guaranteed market for the health insurance, drug industry, and hospital giants. Unfortunately, the Democrats took both the far more efficient, single-payer, full Medicare alternative, which gives people free choice of doctors and hospitals, off the table, as well as the public-option competitor being considered as a part of Obamacare, and rendered them, like Third Party candidates in a presidential debate, invisible.

In regards to the tort system that addresses wrongful injuries, the Democrats are better by far than the endlessly attacking Republicans, but the Democrats continually lack the energy and mojo of the Republican counter-push. However, the Democrats were wholly complicit in the Republican-led escalation of the tough-on-crime legislation and the dead-end war on drugs that has filled our prisons with nonviolent offenders and spawned an industry in private prisons that are operated for profit and with little conscience.

Neither political party has, robust democracy-advocacy program to encourage the shift of power back to the public, from the few to the many—be they communities, citizens, consumers, workers, small taxpayers, or voters. While the

Republicans are messing around with voter suppression, the Democrats are scarcely moving toward a universal voting system such as the one that Australia's people successfully enjoy. Nor are the Democrats challenging the ballot access and voting machine rackets despite the fact that subversive Republican-driven operations have arguably cost Democrats two presidential elections. Indeed, by supporting "top two" winners in the primary referenda in California and Washington State, the two parties have driven out other candidates from being able to participate in general elections. Despite major public opinion in its favor, giving voters the ultimate electoral choice of a binding "none-of-the-above" option or "no confidence" vote, both the Republicans and Democrats consider even discussing such a matter an unspeakable taboo.

What these fundamental convergences between the two political parties portend is more furor over lesser differences and the inducement of citizens to vote for the least-worse candidate instead of candidates who might actually represent them, their needs, and their community. Many voters feel trapped by the fact that Republicans and Democrats often function as two factions of one party—the pro-corporate party.

Over the years, the privileges and immunities granted to these chartered companies have been extended, primarily by courts. Corporations are legally persons under the law, with rights and powers that far exceed those of human beings. In protest against the enormous political distortion this creates, MIT scholar Noam Chomsky writes:

> In the 2010 Supreme Court 5–4 decision on Citizens United, Chief Justice Roberts selected a case that could easily have been settled on narrow grounds, and maneuvered the Court into using it for a far-reaching decision that, in effect, permits corporate managers to buy elections directly, instead of using more indirect means . . .
>
> Corporate campaign contributions are a major factor in determining the outcome of elections, and the same is sure to be true of the virtually unlimited advertising for candidates now permitted by the Court. This alone is a significant factor in policy decisions, reinforced by the enormous power of corporate lobbies and other conditions imposed by the very small sector of the population that dominates the economy.[15]

However we look at it, the wealthy few use the relentless mechanism of commercialism to trample democracy, the natural environment, and the common good. Our grievances are many, and the power of citizenship, community, and national pride should be enough to mobilize the population to organize resistance and change.

THREE

HOW THE SYSTEM IS RIGGED

In recent decades a huge vein of wealth has opened up to privatization: the treasuries of federal, state, and local governments; massive public resources known as the commons; public education; as well as many other community institutions. Uniquely, when the corporatists are unable to gain *ownership* of a resource—turning it into real estate or another disposable product—they instead turn to *control* the resource. In few areas is this more apparent than in the private commercialization of a great public resource—the airwaves.

From the beginning of the radio and television age in the 1920s and '30s, the public airwaves have belonged to the people. The airwaves, their public ownership, and the public interest regulation that was enacted to protect them, present a modern day, information-age example of a "commons." This vast national resource, owned by us all, is administrated by the Federal Communications Commission (FCC), whose job it is to allocate portions of the broadcast spectrum to licensed radio and TV stations that abide by its rules and regulations.

I'm a co-owner of the airwaves, just as you are. One recent Saturday, I turned on the television to see how our public property was being used by NBC, Fox, ABC, CBS, and other over-the-air networks. And what did I see on TV this Saturday afternoon? *Poppy Cat*, *Tree Fu Tom*, *Astroblast*, the *Chica Show*, *World of Adventure Sports*, action sports, track and field championships, infomercials, golf, U.S. Senior Open (5 hours on Fox), infomercials (2.5 hours on ABC), *World of X-Games*, ESPN *Sports Sunday*, *Into the Wild and Exploration*, infomercials, *The Insider*, and PGA Tour Golf —a fairly typical Saturday afternoon on TV, USA.

Hello! Is that all there is for America? And who decides that our common property is only for commercial entertainment, and often second-class entertainment at that, garnished by relentless advertisements and mind-numbing infomercials? Isn't there anything else going on in this country that people may wish to see in order to better learn, aspire, judge, act, and connect with others? I, however, have asked around and have had trouble finding anyone who actually watches Saturday afternoon network television. Obviously, many people must be watching because the networks draw huge streams of revenue from advertisers who pay handsomely for the opportunity to influence viewers.

The FCC is asleep at the wheel in regards to its own charter's obligation and mandate to regulate the airwaves in the public interest. Absent any over-the-air Howard Stern–type obscenities or lewdness, the FCC has been reshaped by the corporate sector to administer the renewal of licenses to big business every eight years for free! That's right; the broadcast television plutocrats have invested heavily in lobbyists and election campaigns to make sure Congress compels the FCC to give our property away 24 hours a day, 365 days a year. Did we ever have a chance to debate this or vote on it? What do we get in return for the billions of dollars earned by big businesses by controlling our property?

Well, an earlier FCC Chairman, Newton Minow, answered that in 1961. He called television "a vast wasteland." What would he think today? He'd wonder what ever happened to the 1934 Communications Act that established the public airwaves as something of a public trust. That is because 47 U.S.C. § 307 requires all licensed stations to perform in the "public convenience, interest or necessity." What was meant by those words was left up to the FCC—a merry-go-round agency where broadcast and cable executives and lawyers join for a tour of duty before returning to their industry with an enhanced resumé.

In better times, the FCC served the public with clearer, non-commercial goals. For example, it upheld observation of the Fairness Doctrine whereby stations had to provide airtime to discuss two or more sides of an issue of community significance, and to also provide the right to on-air replies to personal attacks or political endorsements. These strictures had so many loopholes that they were really just exhortations, but with some effect. "The necessity for the Fairness Doctrine," writes Steve Rendall of the media watchdog group Fairness and Accuracy in Reporting, "arises from the fact that there are many fewer broadcast licenses than people who would like to have them. Unlike publishing, where the tools of the trade are in more or less endless supply, broadcasting licenses are limited by the finite number of available frequencies. Thus, as trustees of a scarce public resource, licensees accept certain public interest obligations in exchange for the exclusive use of limited public airwaves."[16] The Fairness Doctrine was rescinded in 1987 by the FCC under former actor and radio personality Ronald Reagan—one of the many little chocolates he left on the pillow for America's One Percent.

After the gift from the Great Communicator, plutocrats pursuing profit through commercial media have felt no responsibility to reflect the spirit of the 1934 Communications Act, no obligation to provide views that point anywhere beyond their advertisers' products. These commercialists made the "vast wasteland" more vast with watered-down "news" broadcasts bedecked with "fluff." Were an extraterrestrial to visit our great nation and just watch TV, it would likely conclude we were a violent people (cop shows) of chronic giggles (comedies), bulging eyes (thrillers), and watering mouths (junk food ads).

With the advent of scores of cable stations fighting for ever smaller audiences, there still is not a channel for civic activities and accomplishment, not a channel for deeply informing and organizing workers, consumers, taxpayers, or students—totaling all of us—in any serious context. Senator Bernie Sanders repeatedly says, "They [the small billionaire class] want it all." Perhaps the serious people in our country, who number in the many millions, have lost much of their appetite for the mental junk food that commercial television spews out and therefore do not see themselves as having a sufficient stake to object or demand more compelling and motivating use of their common property, the airwaves. They do not demand of it what they do of their national parks, roads, and bridges, though the airwaves are theirs no less than Yosemite National Park or the Grand Canyon. As we do not—and would not—tolerate corporations taking over our libraries, so too should we should not tolerate them controlling our airwaves.

And so the vicious circle becomes an ever-downward spiral. And the remaining programs of substance—such as *60 Minutes* (CBS) or, moving over to PBS, the *Frontline* series—seem more luminous only because of the expansive sea of darkness around them. When the "commons" known as PBS and NPR formed fifty years or so ago, they were deemed necessary to provide informative content that was not expected to be on the commercial networks. This reduced the pressure on the networks and affiliated local stations to ascertain the information needs of their communities and report accordingly. Moreover, in the intervening years, as viewers and listeners of PBS and NPR know too well, the sponsorship from commercial firms has augmented the budgets of these non-profit media. Such funding is just crumbs for One Percenters like the Koch brothers, but a lifeline for those who have no other way to get a real piece of the pie. Needless to say, relying on money from Exxon or the Koch brothers serves to subtly blunt the sharp inquiring edge of hard-hitting programming and minimize the public interest potential of these institutions that were so expected by founders such as Alfred Friendly. In the cold war between public and private interests, plutocracy offers democracy death by a thousand cuts: greed for profits becomes a form of capital punishment.

To those who object to these general characterizations with examples of good programming, I reply that producing features on a diverse range of civic and political activities is far below NPR's and PBS's funder-friendly range of entertaining programs. On weekends, to counter the commercial vapidity and the ditto-head Sunday interview shows, PBS and NPR are just not there. They simply do not look for, or listen to, the rumble of people who are on the ground, acting with conscience, organizing to break through power. Meanwhile, smaller programs—such as *Democracy Now* with Amy Goodman—are picking up the slack of these larger outlets, despite their comparably modest budgets and staff size.

A left/right proposal that I helped to make in 1991 at a special House Committee hearing chaired by Congressman Edward Markey (D–MA), involved an *audience network*. The idea is to make better use of our own airwaves—an essential part of the national commons—and revert some of our daily time to an organized TV network directly representing and accountable to the viewers and listeners. The notion was vigorously opposed by the broadcasting industry and was dropped. A similar hearing in the Senate reached the same fate with several senators parading their denunciations before a crowd of pleased commercial broadcasters from their states.

One time I accused the bloviating Rush Limbaugh of being on corporate welfare. His radio stations are using our property for free, thereby making it easier for Limbaugh to receive $35 million a year for his torrent of ranting inaccuracies that go unchallenged and un-rebutted by any use of the long-gone Fairness Doctrine. Whether feigned or not, Rush seemed not to understand what I was talking about.

That's how deeply ingrained the private exploitation

of our common property is these days, free of charge, by the One Percent who have succeeded in gaining near total control of national resources while operating in bald non-compliance with the mandate that the airwaves be used in the public interest. If One Percenters could somehow make money from advertisers in the Library of Congress or in Yellowstone National Park, they would, because they have done exactly that with our great national treasure, the airwaves.

Of course, apart from some committed intellectuals like Robert W. McChesney and groups like Free Press, Prometheus Radio Project, or Fairness and Accuracy in Reporting, very little public resistance has been organized to dislodge the commercialists from our airwaves. The national expectation level is near zero—a level likely achieved from the numbing effect that years of relentless commercial programming can have on the mind and conscience.

When I ran for President of the United States, I would often speak at large public rallies about the need to charge corporations rent for their private use of our public airwaves; and I'd propose that we'd use their rent to fund an audience network with producers, reporters, studios, and audience participation around the country. In response to these ideas, people would often give me an approving but bemused facial reaction. This is the same kind of zero expectation level regarding common ownership that not only enables the transfer of resources from the many to the few, but that also makes the corporate takeover of everyday life seem perfectly American and normal, like life in the little town that the Disney Corporation fabricated, Celebration, Florida.

My point is that expectation levels—what Abraham

Lincoln called the all-important "public sentiment"—need to change in order to win back control of society from the One Percenters and the corporations that will continue to contaminate the Earth until it is poisoned, let it warm until it is barren, and who will lie until they are caught and brought to justice. Expectation levels need to rise, and public sentiments need to be stoked to enact policy that moves us closer to the kind of society we deserve. The wealthy, of course, will budget whatever it takes to push back with their lawyers, politicians, and PR consultants. My point is sharply illustrated by some raging reactions by earlier business apologists to proposals that started to prevail in our country's past.

On the abolition of children from working in dungeon mines and factories instead of going to public schools, Clarence E. Martin, president of the American Bar Association said that such laws are "a communistic effort to nationalize children . . . it appears to be a definite positive plan to destroy the Republic and substitute a social democracy."

Regarding Social Security: Silas Strawn, former President of the U.S. Chamber of Commerce, called it part of President Franklin D. Roosevelt's attempt to "Sovietize the country."

In regards to the many benefits of a national Medicare system, Harry E. Northam, Director of the Association of American Physicians, declared: "We oppose the Medicare program because foreign experience has shown that socialized medicine is harmful to both the doctor and the patient, primarily to the patient. He suffers most."

At the time when such comments were made they were

seen as coarse but ones that the masses were used to hearing as the normal pronouncements of the ruling classes. Today, the nation suffers through a similar level of crass opposition and organized tantrums in response to President Obama's very watered-down Affordable Care Act. Republican political leaders did their best to sabotage passage of the act, and made every possible argument to convince Americans that it was the product of bad, big government.

On occasion, people in power will sing a new tune once absolutely compelled to do so. In 1967 Henry Ford II declared angrily that if the government's safety standards were imposed, it "would shut down the industry." A decade later, in 1977, on NBC's *Meet the Press*, Mr. Ford recognized, "We wouldn't have had the kinds of safety built into automobiles that we have had unless there had been a federal law."

More often, the obsession with accruing profit is so overwhelming that commercialists scheme like street criminals to cheat the law, their customers, and society as a whole. Such was the case with Volkswagen when the conscious decision was made to manufacture a car that was programmed to deceive emissions tests. "There was a tolerance for breaking the rules," confessed Hans Dieter Pötsch, head of Volkswagen's supervisory board, at a news conference in December 2015.[17] Spot checks found that some Volkswagen models could spew more than 40 times the allowable limit of nitrogen oxide on the open road, but were programmed to comply with U.S. environmental standards only when subjected to an emissions laboratory test. Volkswagen produced 11 million cars that were rigged to cheat. The air we breathe is also a precious "commons," and when Volkswagen made the decision to rig its cars, it chose to treat our air like a filthy sewer.

In addition to the airwaves, the other great tangible commons belonging to the American people is the onshore public lands that constitute one-third of the nation's territorial mass. Again, they are owned by the people, but unless explicitly protected as national parks or monuments, there is constant pressure on federal agencies by timber, grazing, and mining industries for these national treasures to be plundered for private profit.

It is difficult to overstate how the relentless drive to excavate what is on and under our lands has left behind all forms of wreckage and ruin—toxic, radioactive, and biological. It is hard to describe the long-term consequences of the massive clear-cutting of virgin trees, including the majestic redwoods and spruces, the vast areas of soil erosion and stream damage, the huge piles of mineral wastes, including radioactive uranium tailings, the contamination of water, the destruction of habitats for animals that seriously affect the balance of nature, the ruination of the prairies, and the callous desecration of places held sacred by the indigenous nations and communities who were living here for centuries before European immigrants arrived.

In one of the greatest ongoing surrenders of any country's history, our nation's natural resources have either been given away freely or leased at bargain-basement prices. Unlike any other country in the world, the United States has a law on the books—the 1872 Mining Act—that requires the federal government to give away mining rights, without any royalties in return, to mining companies, domestic or foreign, that discover precious "hard rock" minerals such as gold, silver, and molybdenum. Well, the U.S. does not exactly give away the land; it charges no more than five dollars an acre. Much to the delight of mining giants like American Barrick Resources Corporation of Canada, the fee has never been adjusted for inflation.

According to a 1994 report by the Mineral Policy Institute, Barrick received "patents" on 1,038 acres. The Mineral Policy Center explains that "patent" as follows: "A company that discovers a valuable mineral deposit on its claim can "patent," or gain fee title to, the land for a price not to exceed $5.00 per acre. Upon patent issuance, title to public lands is transferred to private ownership." Barrick "purchased" the 1,038 acres for $5,190 or $5 per acre. Those acres held mineral reserves valued at more than $10 billion![18]

No matter how many times people have described this antiquated law—originally passed to help lone prospectors—the mining lobby has repulsed all sporadic efforts to bring it into the 21st century, such as those attempts by members of Congress like the veteran legislator Nick Rahall, (D-WV) who was defeated in 2014.

For corporations seeking to exploit oil, gas, coal, uranium, trees, or grazing land, the federal government's fees are like a perpetual fire sale. Countries in the developing world charge much more for their natural resources. Uncle Sam has been made into Uncle Sucker by a bunch of rich One Percenters that most Americans have never heard of but to whom they are gifting billions of dollars every year.

With the discovery of oil in Alaska in the 1960s, communities there made sure their lawmakers protected them and established the Alaska Permanent Fund, which annually distributes dividends to each child, woman, and man in that state out of the royalties the oil companies pay to exploit the people's commons. Back in the 1960s, it took just a few political leaders, some good newspapers, an aroused public, and presto—it was done! If this effort were initiated today, it is very doubtful that the legislature in Juneau, now heavily marinated in oil, would be inclined to enact such a far-seeing measure. This is an example of what is meant by the right move at the right time by a few people.

There is considerable political and regional opposition to the very idea of preserving the public lands by limiting the range of the extractors and the developers. The more extreme among these privatizers want most of the public lands to be turned into real estate and opened to commercialization. They present a more powerful force to be reckoned with by politicians than the unorganized tide of public opinion that is opposed to their designs. But the pressures of the privatizers, even when unsuccessful, have collateral effects such as reducing budgets to slow down and restore horrible soil erosion or to adequately fund the national parks. The entire system of the fifty-eight national parks—including Yosemite, Yellowstone, and Shenandoah National Parks—has a yearly budget of around 2.6 billion dollars, or one-fifth of the cost of one new aircraft carrier.

Corporatization—or "privatization," as those who benefit from it prefer to say—is the process used to commercialize and extract profit from as much of society as possible: from public water systems, from public schools, from control of the Internet, from national parks, non-profit hospitals, and even from some fire departments. These commons are seen as lucrative resources to be tapped, no matter the local consequences, and then abandoned the moment they've been picked clean. The drive for such conversions is getting bolder and wider into areas long held off-limits to business.

And in many cases, the risks to families, communities, and the natural environment are immense. For example, the blind rush to frack Oklahoma dry of its fossil fuels has ushered in waves of earthquakes so frequent and severe that even the business journal *Bloomberg*, issued a sobering article in October 2015 sounding the alarm that "Oklahoma earthquakes are a national security threat" which could prove to be an even "bigger risk" than terrorism.[19] So serious is the situation, pro-corporate *Bloomberg* even felt compelled to note that "Energy firms tried to slow science inquiries blaming them for earthquakes in Oklahoma."[20] The state now suffers through, on average, at least 2 earthquakes per day, some of which have measured at magnitudes of 4.7 and 4.8. Oklahoma endured 907 quakes in 2015, a 50 percent increase from 2014. Despite this, and the direst warnings about the impact of fossil fuel on catastrophic climate change, the profit-driven stampede to frack the fuel out of the ground continues at full throttle. "With no explicit authority to regulate seismic issues," reported the *New York Times* in early 2016, the Oklahoma Corporation Commission, which oversees the industry, attempted to persuade frackers to "voluntarily follow a series of ever-stricter directives on waste disposal in earthquake zones."[21] Good luck! Meanwhile, seismologists safely monitoring the situation from the National Earthquake Information Center in Colorado are all expecting a "big one" soon.

In addition to the ruination of land, corporations have no compunction about ruining our schools as well. Years ago the Rand Corporation laid out a plan for moving in on a public school market that was then worth 300 billion dollars a year. When such moves succeed, they not only manage to gain increasing control of public budgets, but also diminish the non-commercial spirit of education. Once infiltrated, schools slowly become compromised as educational sites where the "everything is for sale" directive of the marketplace creeps in to influence children's minds.

One of the flimsiest corporate arguments made to defend commercialization of public resources is that it somehow saves the taxpayers money. Tell that to Admiral Hyman Rickover, who for years urged a U.S. Navy-owned shipyard to demonstrate what he believed to be excessive costs of corporate shipbuilders to U.S. taxpayers.[22]

Tell that to the Pentagon and Medicare auditors and the Government Accountability Office (GAO) of Congress, documenting hundreds of billions of dollars in annual waste, fraud, and abuses in the marketplace. Nonetheless, the indentured members of Congress run with this corporatization myth and repeatedly ensure that outsourcing happens and their campaign cash swells. Of course, it doesn't help when public institutions like schools do not perform at acceptable levels, for example, or when they are so underfunded that they become vulnerable to pitches for quick fixes that bring commercial marketing, advertising, and influence where democracy-centered society does not want it to be. This makes schools and communities vulnerable to the commercial sector instead of maintaining civic vigilance and pursuing reforms that maintain the original commitments to public education standards.

Corporations have managed to stall or over-run Congress, many state legislatures, and their respective executive branches, and have turned to capturing the remaining branch of government—the courts. The judiciary has long presented problems for corporate buccaneers who pay to play. There were just too many courts, too many juries, too many judges appointed for life, too many public testimonies open to the media, and too many adversarial subpoenas and cross-examinations to influence with the usual behind-closed-doors maneuvering.

Conquering the courts was an expensive pursuit because many bases had to be covered. The drive was anything but slapdash or random, and involved much more than just responding to losses here and there. There were two general goals: first, to obstruct access to judicial justice for ordinary people who are wrongfully injured or defrauded by corporate practices; and second, to make it easier for corporations to win those cases that do manage to make it all the way to the courts' dockets.

Both of these objectives were often planned and argued by corporate attorneys or the lobbyists whom they trained. For both federal and state courts, budgets have been cut. At the federal judiciary, drug cases took up so much of the courts' time that civil jury trials were delayed, squeezed out, or unduly pressured by judges to settle. From the U.S. Supreme Court to the District Courts, all federal courts throughout the nation have to make do on funding about the size of the Congressional budget—approximately $6.7 billion. On average, about two percent of states' budgets go to state courts. With grossly inadequate resources available for those in need of a public defender or some form of legal aid, caseloads decline and plea agreements, under duress, increase sharply.

Then there has been the campaign to elect pro-business judges. The Texas Supreme Court is a case in point. Up until the end of the 1970s, the Court was a leader in expanding the rights of people to use the law of torts to address their grievous injuries. The corporatists launched a money drive to elect their sympathizers to the court and within less than a decade, the Texas Supreme Court became so squeamishly pro-corporate that some of the remaining fair-minded Justices resigned in disgust. At the same time, the corporate-led war against Workers, Compensation, and the common law of medical malpractice and product liability was won again and again in the corporate-bred legislature in Austin, Texas. Never mind the facts showing the need for strengthening these safeguards.

Using falsehoods to finance and win a statewide referendum in 2003 to strip the Texas Constitution of its prohibition of damage caps on what juries could decide was a far-reaching and radical business *coup-d'état* on the independence of the judiciary. To make matters worse, business interests continue to pay for a lobby called "Texans Against Lawsuit Abuse," modeled on other similar groups in many other states. Tying the hands of judges and juries under corporate-greased legislative restrictions ends up tying the hands of wronged people seeking justice one case at a time before an impartial tribunal. Unfortunately the Texas plaintiff's bar would not provide enough of the necessary resources and smart strategies to stay in contention.

Attorneys hired by One Percenters and corporations did not stop there. They erected elaborate procedural obstacles that could wear and tear down plaintiffs and their lawyers after they file suit in court. In a brilliant description of these powerful procedural blockages in the federal courts, New York University law professor Arthur Miller, the leading procedural expert on the federal courts, personally described his own dismay over what has happened in the last fifty years when the federal rules of civil procedures went from facilitating use of the courts to blocking the ability of plaintiffs—either as individuals or as class actions—to have their cases tried on the merits. As a result, the people's right to have their day in court is being foreclosed.

Corporate victories in federal and state elections work hand in hand with this mission by assuring the nomination of more commercially-responsive judges such as Chief Justice Roberts, and Justices Scalia and Alito, with the same being true in many states. More than one corporate lawyer has said that they "do not practice law, they practice judge."

One ingenious way that corporations have successfully blocked people's access to the courts has been the way they have, over the years, eliminated people's freedom of contract. We've all signed on the dotted line; today we click "I Agree" without even scrolling through the blur of fine print that establishes contract servitude or contract peonage. Thousands of law students are taught that freedom of contract is a major pillar of private American law, yet they spend less than two hours of class time on these fine-print contracts. (Senator Elizabeth Warren calls them "mice type" contracts.) The rest of the required course on contracts is devoted to "negotiated" contracts between businesses or with government and unionized labor participants who can negotiate with each other knowledgeably.

Here is how corporations use contracts to maximize themselves and minimize you. If you buy insurance, cars, fuel, computer services; if you shop for credit, home mortgages, hospitals, airline or train tickets, hotel rooms, savings or brokerage accounts, summer camps, rental products and services, express mail service, or sign apartment rental or business leases—if you purchase any of these then you're likely to be giving away your right to go to court for your grievances. It's called the compulsory arbitration clause from which there is no appeal, except for fraud by the arbitrators. After you sign, your right to reject whatever additional costs, penalties, or even change the terms that your vendor chooses to make, is taken away by a "unilateral modification" clause. These are just two of the truly remarkable acts of legal domination and surrender that occur the moment you sign or click on "I Agree."

No government can take away your right to your day in court. But corporations can and do. No contract can be called a contract when only one side is able to change the terms; but judges say that it's okay and cite the myth that you gave your consent. Even law professors have admitted they often do not read the fine print of some contracts when they purchase goods and services, because it is futile to try to make any changes.

Try not consenting. Make a few changes like doubling the warranty period or deleting your vendor's waiver of liability. Initial your changes in the margins. Then hand the signed contract back to the salesperson. When, over forty years ago, some people handed over our own printed consumer's agreement in the process of buying a new car, one dealer called the police. Another one chased the customer out the door shouting, "You dirty communist."

There is collective bargaining by unions with management; but there is no collective bargaining by consumers for terms on purchasing cars, mortgages, insurance, or credit cards. So silently, so relentlessly has this contract servitude expanded that young people, even self-avowed libertarians, don't even think twice about consenting to these corporate dictators. Consent is manufactured. So tyrannical are these fine-print dictates that a leading legal scholar, Professor Margaret Radin, suggested that these contracts should be considered a wrongful injury themselves, or a tort.

Consider patients who survive medical malpractice and are blocked from exercising their right to trial by jury in a court of law. Or the millions of American families plunged into crisis, or worse—foreclosure—because of some inscrutable fine print in the terms of their mortgage. They'll understand what Margaret Radin meant. Our country, from the beginning, emphasized "freedom of contract" as a major liberating doctrine. Corporations and One Percenters pay lawyers handsomely to override that principle every day.

Unconscionable clauses buried in the fine print of contracts, and unilateral updates to mortgage servicing agreements or credit card terms are almost always adverse to the customer. The vendor-supplied contract has many whips. Once you buy with a credit card, the seller can overbill you, charge you for services you never requested, and impose outrageous penalties and late fee charges that drive profits higher for big business. Should you object, you risk a lowered credit rating and credit scores which can expose you to denials of credit far removed from your vendor or to higher interest rates and onerous terms and conditions. Lobbyists hired by finance companies in the 1970s helped abolish pro-consumer state usury laws that put a ceiling on interest rates, so that corporate loan sharks can roll your debt over and add hundreds of percent to the original amount borrowed. These practices are common in the payday loan and installment loan rackets.

When phone companies rip off customers by billing them for things they never ordered it is called "cramming"—a crime defined by the FCC as "the illegal act of placing unauthorized charges on your wireline, wireless, or bundled services telephone bill." This particular form of corporate theft has been perpetrated against millions of American households.[23]

Creditors can sue you in small claims court, as they do in New York, and those who are supposed to serve the summons often just throw it away so you don't know to show up in court and therefore get a default judgment against you. Small claims courts are now often dominated by bill collectors and other vendors. One Percenters and their henchmen play with the laws as if they were so much inventory. The customer scarcely knows what they are being denied or how they are being controlled. They rarely realize how they could have been given better products and services, as well as better health, safety, and corporate fraud deterrence that would make vendors perform less deceptively. Public education often ignores such manipulations because they are too controversial to handle.

The legal profession and law schools often fail as first responders, so far that is. The double standard in the way the law and the courts treat the rich and powerful compared to the rest of us is widely perceived from all quarters of American society. The gross imbalance is more than just the majority of the country being economically unable to spare the income necessary to employ lawyers to fight back for them. For example, pressing for prosecution of Wall Street's criminal bankers probably has a ninety-percent support among Americans. But it just did not happen. There is a whole vernacular among regular people about this double standard. "The rich get off, the poor get put away." "He'll get off with a slap on the wrist." "If you can pay for fancy lawyers, the law won't get you." This folk understanding was reiterated recently by Matt Taibbi in *Rolling Stone* when he wrote, "Americans have long understood that the rich get good lawyers and get off, while the poor suck eggs and do time . . . An arrestable class and an unarrestable class."[24]

Petty theft can get you sent away for several years in some places, but looting billions from pensions, exposing workers to lethal toxins or dangerous work conditions, or knowingly not recalling motor vehicles with fatal defects, lands few One Percenters in handcuffs, and fewer in prison. Crime in the streets is news nightly, while crime in the suites is taboo. The few lower-level corporate criminals who do get prosecuted, convicted, and incarcerated find themselves in short-term country-club prisons.

According to Russell Mokhiber, editor of the *Corporate Crime Reporter*, "Corporate crime takes far more lives, causes far more injuries and diseases and steals far more money than street crime, but the vast amount of law enforcement resources, mass media attention and prison cell blocks are devoted to street crime."

Just consider these preventable casualties: almost 60,000 annual workplace-related fatalities from both disease and trauma (Occupational Safety & Health Administration); 54,000 deaths a year from air pollution (Environmental Protection Agency); over 100,000 lives lost as a result of medical malpractice (Harvard School of Public Health Studies); nearly 100,000 lives lost from hospital-induced infections (Centers for Disease Control); over 100,000 fatalities from adverse effects of drugs; and over 40,000 deaths yearly due to inadequate or no healthcare coverage for diagnosis, treatment, and medication. There are far larger numbers of sicknesses and injuries attached to these data sets.

These statistics have haunting human faces: children, women, men, and families destroyed by uncontrolled monetized minds. Whether they are caused by recklessness, criminal negligence, or worse, the key factors in common are the *preventability* of such pain, and the suffering inflicted from commercially induced neglect, predation, manslaughter, and homicide. By comparison, street and home homicides do not exceed 14,000 lives lost annually.

Now see how companies have made sure they have the laws that they need to go after you; and how they make sure the law can be used as their punisher. The giant, multi-tiered home mortgage business, now driven by the same One Percenters who profited from crashing the economy in 2008–2009, can nail you if you misrepresent information on your mortgage application. Suppose you say you're going to occupy your house as a principal residence to get a lower interest rate and down-payment, and you don't for some reason. Lenders can call the loan and demand repayment if the mortgage balance is outstanding. Absent that payment, the lender can seize your home—foreclosure. In addition, by claiming you committed bank fraud, these companies can use the FBI against you. As the veteran housing columnist Kenneth R. Harvey warned, this can trigger severe financial penalties, prosecution, and prison time for ordinary Americans. But how many bankers feel the cold metal of handcuffs tighten on their wrists when their crimes rob American families of their homes and life savings?

Health insurance companies have similar supporting laws to deny medical coverage by alleging "illegal activities." This could mean anything from non-disclosure of traffic violations to gun accidents, even when there have been no convictions. It could mean something as vague as "hazardous" behavior, according to the *New York Times*. If a company paid you and comes back for their money, they can get you prosecuted for fraud.

These corporate goliaths are too big to fail. But they know how to enact laws to make sure you are too small to stop them.

Corporate state culture—the plutocracy cum oligarchy—is given an astonishing exoneration so long as it claims that violence and mayhem are not their direct purpose but an unfortunate byproduct that couldn't be helped. Like when innocent people are accidentally killed by U.S. drone attacks, the government seems to quietly get a free pass. It is almost as if corporations get away with a permanent defense of institutional insanity, a defense going global in terms of deadly supply chains, from horrific African mines to dangerous factories in China, India and Bangladesh; deoxygenation and poisoning of the vast oceans, estuaries, rivers, and lakes; upping greenhouse gasses into rapid climate destabilization; extending the range of infectious diseases due to habitat and ecological disruption and desecration; and changing the nature of nature itself through unregulated genetic engineering and nanotechnology. Even with six million slow, agonizing deaths a year globally attributed to the tobacco business, cigarettes are still demonically promoted by One Percenters who reap staggering profits from selling their addictive and poisonous product, especially in developing nations where regulations protecting children do not exist. The excuse is forever that corporatists have no intention, knowledge, or reason to do harmful things—the institutional insanity defense again.

Or the manufacturers of weapons of mass destruction, whose militant advertisements say they are just helping the national defense, but are not at all responsible for their products' use in the coercive policies of empire and perpetual war. Is it institutional madness or infantilism? Did the World War II Allies let the giant Krupp Works in Germany get away with this excuse after the war ended? It is time for people to take away these rationalizations of omnicide from corporations that demand they be legally privileged as "persons" for their pursuit of profits but not as "persons" for our pursuit of them as criminal predators and fugitives from justice.

In the 2012 U.S. presidential campaign, Republican nominee Mitt Romney, asked about corporate personhood, replied as if it was a given, saying "corporations are people," like it was a science fact he learned in fifth grade. This is no mere throwaway line. Billions of dollars of litigating, advertising, marketing, and corporatist commentary have been focused on driving this "people" image into our minds from childhood. Regularly, full-page ads show that goliath corporations, such as Walmart or Lockheed Martin, are just people—like you. The ads are filled with pictures and names of the faithful workers who bring you their goods and services.

But these loyal employees have no say whatsoever when their bosses shut down and move their worksite to Asia or Central America. They have no say when corporate algorithms determine that what's now best is for their full-time schedule to be scaled down to part-time work with irregular hours, wreaking havoc on family schedules, as was the case with Walmart and its employees, for example. They have no say when they learn that their pensions have been looted and their private retirement security is gone. They have no say when they're exposed to dangerous or toxic workplace conditions that sicken them. They have no say when the huge profits derived from the sweat of their brow is used, not for productive investment or increased wages, but to buy back the company stock that produces nothing except ever higher compensation for their plutocratic bosses.

Standing before the CEO of Exxon/Mobil a few years ago, the lawyer, prominent investor advocate, and author, Robert Monks, asked why, at the annual shareholders meeting, the big boss did not call himself Emperor. So obviously, corporations are very different kinds of "people." As they become bigger and more globally evasive, they also become more dominant over the lives of the people that they employ, more dominant over capital and technology. At the same time, they also exhibit an increasing ability to be both destructive and immune to the kinds of deterrence, law, and justice that 99 percent of the population is compelled to obey. The top 200 global corporations now have combined sales that are often equivalent to over 25 percent of the world's GDP. In 1976 Morton Mintz and Jerry Cohen, writing in their classic book, *Power, Inc.*, called these business entities private governments.

Given the continued concentration of corporate profit and power since then, the phrase "private government" seems almost quaint. Global corporate government is more like what is happening—sidestepping, buying, or pitting public governments against one another so that they let CEOs have their way.

What does a "global corporation" entail beyond buying and selling, investing or disinvesting globally in dozens of countries and all the continents on Earth? It means striving to overcome all civic and political obstacles to the mounting growth of sales, profits, stock value and executive compensation. In the early 20th century, Marine General Smedley Butler, double Congressional Medal of Honor winner, and author of *War Is a Racket* (1935), asserted that arrogant big companies got the Marines dispatched to put down local resistance and revolts or topple popular regimes in South America and Asia. After World War II, that meant spreading out to the entire developing world with open or clandestine expeditions to overturn about fifty regimes deemed a threat to U.S. business interests under the camouflage of going after left-leaning governments. Guatemala's elected leader in 1954 and Iran's elected prime minister in 1953 learned about combined government/corporate power the hard way, as did their people, after being overthrown by U.S. plots and replaced by brutal dictators, for being nationalist champions of their country's essential economic assets.

Under the dictatorial yoke of the IMF and the World Bank—most heavily influenced by its leading funder, the United States—debt traps could be used to ensnare nations to Western banks, and severe wage austerity could be used to further squeeze their already impoverished populations. What have been euphemistically called "structural adjustments" were imposed on these countries: cuts in food production and subsidies for the poor, conversion of land from domestic use to cash crops for export, tax cuts for the wealthy, and cuts in funds to maintain critical public facilities and infrastructure.

Military alliances such as NATO and SEATO provided U.S. arms industries with huge ongoing orders for aircraft, tanks, missiles, fighting ships, and other advanced killing machines. Corporate support for foreign aid was based on American taxpayer money going to countries such as Israel, Egypt, and Pakistan to use to buy weapons from U.S. businesses on favorable terms. Our government's insurer of U.S. investment abroad, known as OPIC (the Overseas Private Investment Corporation), and the Export/Import Bank of the United States, provide loan guarantees for exports by giants like Boeing, and further privilege the Washington-guaranteed position of our global tax-escaping corporations abroad.

With corporations always on the lookout for securing larger shares of global control, the modern "free trade treaty" came into play to serve that end. Previous trade agreements between nations to reduce trade tariffs, quotas, and other barriers were essentially voluntary. The recent versions, starting with the enforceable North American Free Trade Agreement (NAFTA), then the larger World Trade Organization (WTO) and the pending Trans-Pacific Partnership (TPP), are draconian penalty-equipped instruments intended to subordinate domestic mechanisms for protecting consumers, workers, and the environment to the supremacy of "trade." In addition, these treaties required secret tribunals to resolve disputes between nations, thereby bypassing open courts and the local laws they uphold. Within the secret tribunals, corporate trade lawyers, serving as temporary judges, can have their decisions enforced so that the losing nation must either repeal their domestic laws and regulations or pay substantive fines to the prevailing country.

For example, in 2015 the WTO's tribunal in Geneva, Switzerland, ruled that the United States would have to repeal its popular "country of origin" labeling requirement for meat sold in retail stores or pay meat exporters in Brazil and Mexico up to $1 billion in fines. The U.S. House of Representatives could hardly wait to repeal its own law and deprive the vast majority of American consumers the right to know where the meat they buy comes from. The consumer law was repealed by Congress because of an edict of a secret tribunal. Were these corporate-managed trade treaties in place when we were pressing for air bags, signatory countries could have attacked this life-saving standard as an unlawful "non-tariff trade barrier," that blocked imports of vehicles produced without this safety device.

Or if we want now to adopt a major new safety feature for motor vehicles, the new policy could be challenged at the WTO and NAFTA. If the standard in question was stronger than that decided upon by a cloistered, corporate-influenced "harmonization committee" of signatory nations, we could face trade sanctions unless and until we eliminate the improvement. If the proposed TPP were to go into effect, U.S. taxpayers might have to pay damages to foreign investors over such policies. These trade agreements prevent our country from being first in the way our consumers, workers, and environment are treated.

Small wonder that genuine conservatives, such as Pat Buchanan, are opposed to this shredding of our sovereignty. Countries, including our own, that care more for their citizens, are the ones most liable to lose before these tribunals in cases brought by nations who have lower, less safe standards. These lagging countries, often hard dictatorships or autocratic oligarchies, don't get in trouble under the WTO's "pull-down" form of autocratic governance. Worse, the WTO allows products made by children forced to work in dungeon-like factories and mines to be exported from developing nations. The United States cannot pass a law prohibiting imports of products under barbarian conditions, competing against U.S. workers under U.S. standards, because such legislation would be considered a trade violation and over-ridden by WTO tribunals. Senator Tom Harkin (D–Iowa) tried to pass just such a bill in 1996. Under Bill Clinton, the White House said to him, "Don't bother, Tom, it would be WTO-illegal and we would lose," meaning we would have to repeal our law or pay huge fines and endure other retaliations. This occurred in modern day America, the nation that banned domestic child labor in 1938 after earlier bans were blocked by the U.S. Supreme Court. Examples abound that demonstrate the corporate subversion and sabotage of democracy.

You may be asking how in the world these trade treaties get through Congress. Three reasons at least. First, they are not called treaties by the White House. Unlike other countries that call them treaties, our presidents strategically classify them as "agreements." Why? Only a fifty-one percent of the vote is needed from the Senate and House to pass "agreements," whereas a two-thirds vote in the Senate is needed to get a "treaty" through. Second, the proposed treaty is sent to the Congress for an up or down vote, under a fast-track procedure that prohibits amendments by any member of Congress and severely restricts the time for debate on the Senate or House floors. Autocratic handcuffing procedures lead to autocratic results. Third, such trade treaties do not at all stick to trade; they are the ultimate stealth deregulating machines. Corporations, whose attorneys draft the terms of these "agreements," love the "open sesame" opportunities to ditch U.S. workers in favor of the abysmally low cost of labor in developing countries where the governments are notoriously corruptible.

Corporations also relish the sidelining of sovereign nations in favor of commercially-dominated tribunals empowered by these treaties. The less these globalist companies have to resolve disputes under more open democratic institutions such as our courts, legislatures, executive branch departments, and regulatory agencies, the more political and economic hegemony they can impose and enjoy. As former World Bank economist Professor Herman Daly said:

> International "free trade pacts" (NAFTA, TPP, TAFTA) are supposed to increase global GDP, thereby making us all richer and effectively expanding the size of the earth and easing conflict. But growth in the full world has become uneconomic—increasing costs faster than benefits. It now makes us poorer, not richer. These secretly negotiated agreements among the elites are designed to benefit private global corporations, often at the expense of the public good of nations. Some think that strengthening global corporations by erasing national boundaries will reduce the likelihood of war. More likely we will just shift to feudal corporate wars in a post-national global commons, with corporate fiefdoms effectively buying national governments and their armies, supplemented by already existing private mercenaries.[25]

Those nations and the companies behind them that

challenge the more humane standards of particular countries and slander them as "non-tariff trade barriers" are slowly using the enforcement tools so as not to rouse the ire of people everywhere to demand that their government exercise the standard six-month notice of withdrawal. The World Trade Organization has over 162 signatory nations, each with just one vote (St. Kitts with 69,000 people has the same single vote as do China, Russia, the United States, and Germany). The European Union, Japan, the United States, and Canada have all issued annual reports listing hundreds of laws and regulations in each other's country they believe to be WTO-illegal. These reports seek to fuel efforts to override local laws that protect dolphins from death by tuna fishing nets, ban special chemicals and additives, and demand that food be labeled in certain ways, as is the case under California law. But signatory nations are moving incrementally to tie up nations inside the World Trade Organization web for fear of provoking a backlash of outrage.

Companies, moreover, are becoming bolder. Under the so-called "nation-state dispute mechanism"—strongly criticized by Senator Elizabeth Warren and defended by President Obama—corporations in one country can take another country to these secret tribunals and demand big money from them by alleging that local regulations protecting safety, labor, and environment have limited or stopped the sale of their products.

Senator Elizabeth Warren is particularly concerned about the Investor-State Dispute Settlement (ISDS) provisions of the Trans-Pacific Partnership (TPP) trade deal. Warren notes the ISDS "doesn't directly tell countries to repeal regulations. It imposes a financial penalty, which has caused countries to change their regulations . . . [ISDS mechanisms] never had the authority to override regulations. What they had was the authority to impose a monetary penalty directly against the government and its taxpayers. That's the point at which governments have backed up and said, 'we can't afford this, we'll just change the law.'"[26]

Public Citizen's Global Trade Watch found that

> more than $440 million in compensation has already been paid out to corporations in a series of investor-state cases under NAFTA-style deals. This includes attacks on natural resource policies, environmental protections, health and safety measures and more. In fact, of the more than $34 billion in the 18 pending claims under NAFTA-style deals, nearly all relate to environmental, energy, financial, public health, land use and transportation policies—not traditional trade issues.[27]

The strategic planning by global corporations to escape the laws and standards of the nation state has been accelerating over the decades. In the 1940s and 1950s, authors wrote about the "Seven Sisters"—the seven largest oil companies and how they created their own global regime. In 1972 Carl A. Gerstacker, chairman of Dow Chemical Company, revealed this yearning by his big-business colleagues. He declared that an "anational corporation," without any national ties, could operate more flexibly and freely around the world. Later he told an inquirer that for a decade, Dow had been studying the possibility of relocating to an island in the Caribbean. The chief obstacle, he added, would be unfavorable tax consequences to investors in the exchange of stock involved in such a corporate emigration.[28]

Escaping the nation state, especially the larger, more formidable states, has been the goal of corporate attorneys for many years. That is what "tax havens" are all about in such accommodating jurisdictions as the Cayman Islands, Ireland, Luxemburg, Bermuda, Switzerland, and Britian's Isle of Man. Tax attorneys have recently conceived of something called "an inversion." This is where a functioning corporation chartered in the United States, like Pfizer, sheds its U.S. citizenship, then acquires and melts into another company chartered, for example, in Ireland or Luxemburg, where tax rates cost the company less. The former U.S. company still maintains its full presence in the United States with its workers, sales, and other operations. But by shuffling papers, the attorneys can get the best of both worlds for the massive corporations that hire them: public services paid for by us, the taxpayers, while contributing fewer tax payments in return. Even the wealthiest One Percenters, with a few exceptions, would think twice about renouncing their U.S. citizenship for a tax deal, but few of them see the hypocrisy of complaining about our government's deficits.

When it comes to taxes, it's truly startling how the freeloading executives of U.S. corporations, so lavishly nurtured for so many years by so many of America's governmental institutions, are unrestrained by any sense of national loyalty or patriotism when they engage in such tax-avoiding flights. Their arrangement allows them to have it both ways: the advantages of our country without the responsibility of contributing to the country's upkeep and security. Most regular taxpayers generally have heard about these "tax loopholes" for the rich. The common reaction is for people to push to get *their* tax burden reduced rather than to go after the variety of gigantic tax reductions that lawyers and lobbyists win for their corporate clients. On December 20, 2015, *The New York Times* reported that it took eleven days for lobbyists hired by billionaire One Percenters, along with allies from the hotel, restaurant, and gambling industries, to successfully add 54 words to a tax and spending bill that would deprive the U.S. Treasury of $1 billion in future federal tax payments.[29]

Since World War II, the percentage of the overall national revenue garnered through the taxation of corporations has been dropping. In 1950, federal corporate tax collections amounted to about thirty percent of all federal revenues. Today it is only seven percent. The highly regarded public interest tax analyst Robert McIntyre, director of Citizens for Tax Justice (CTJ), rebuts the propaganda that the United States has the highest corporate taxes in the developed world. He makes the distinction between the thirty-five percent nominal *rate* and what rigging the tax code does for these companies' *actual* payments to Uncle Sam. He writes: "in practice, the true U.S. corporate tax rate is barely half of the thirty-five percent nominal rate . . . the biggest and most profitable Fortune 500 corporations paid only 18.5 percent in federal income taxes on their U.S. profits from 2008 through 2010. Many companies paid little or nothing."[30]

Which ones paid nothing? McIntyre reported that during the five-year period between 2008 and 2012, 26 commercial corporations, including Boeing, General Electric and Verizon, paid no federal income taxes. That means a high-school student getting paid minimum wage at Taco Bell contributed more dollars to the upkeep of the nation than all of these massive corporations combined.[31]

Ninety-three other corporations paid an effective tax rate of less than ten percent over the same period. Of the 280 companies Citizens for Tax Justice studied, 111 paid zero in federal income taxes for at least one year between 2008 and 2012. Astonishingly, some very profitable companies, such as General Electric, have been able to receive *from* the U.S. Treasury hundreds of millions of dollars in any one year. Such are the grotesque and contrived intricacies of the tax laws. "Phantom costs" never incurred, indefinite deferral of U.S. taxes on their offshore profits, and the purchase of other companies' tax liabilities are some of the obscure methods that result in corporate tax attorneys getting praise and fat annual bonuses. Over the first decade of the 21st century, General Electric averaged a federal income tax rate of only 2.3 percent on its 83 billion dollars in U.S. profits. This huge tax escapee and major job exporter, General Electric, has such political influence that President Obama picked its CEO, Jeffrey Immelt, to chair the President's Council on Jobs and Competitiveness. This deplorable cushy relationship between big business and big government extends, of course, to Congress, where McIntyre found that in 2012, "ninety-eight percent of sitting members of Congress have accepted campaign money from the thirty most notorious tax avoiding companies." Boeing is one of them. During the new century's first ten years, Boeing only paid federal income taxes in two years (2002 and 2007) and has gotten bizarre tax refunds from the U.S. Treasury all the other years (in addition to muscling out of paying Washington state taxes). Now for the kicker: McIntyre calculates that Boeing's average federal tax rate during that decade was at *negative* 6.5 percent.[32]

You want a sense of place for the fleeing corporations? Last year I stood in front of Ugland House, a nondescript five-story building in the Cayman Islands that has found room for the registered addresses of 18,857 companies! Paper registrations, with a post office box, don't take up much space. But are they ever lucrative for the many subsidiaries of the big banks, insurance companies, and other global corporations, for the Grand Cayman Island extract no income tax from them. You can see once again how different corporations are from us and how nearly impossible it is to have equal justice under the law with such massive inequalities in power, privilege, and profits.[33]

Over 2 trillion dollars in U.S. corporate profits—including the result of phony profit-shifting "transfer pricing"—rest unproductively in these tax havens. To drive his many points home to tens of millions of small taxpayers, McIntyre declares: "Every dollar in taxes companies avoid by using tax havens must be balanced by higher taxes paid by other Americans, cuts to government programs, or increased federal debt."[34]

One Percenters were not standing idly by as they saw what their large corporations could get away with by keeping the tax man away. They made sure their capital gains and dividends, called "unearned income" by the tax law, were taxed at a much lower rate than the income of ordinary people. Such laws help the rich get richer, and helps widen the gulf between them and the rest of the nation.

In the second term of the George W. Bush administration, the wealthy had almost all the Republican members of Congress behind scrapping the venerable, already loophole-riddled estate tax. Their lobbying campaign even replaced the words "estate tax" with "death tax," leading one opponent of such transmissions of trillions of dollars of wealth tax-free to their recipients to quip, "better to tax the dead than to tax the living." They wanted abolition of the federal estate tax that was imposed only on estates above $5 million, with married couples being able to double that exemption.[35]

The repeal probably would have been enacted were it not for the remarkable opposition and mobilization of some rich people of conscience: George Soros, Abigail Disney, Jimmy Carter, and even Robert Rubin of Citigroup notoriety who, as Clinton's Secretary of the Treasury, set into motion the deregulation of Wall Street.[36] Organized wealthy people, led by William Gates Sr. of United for a Fair Economy, put out rebuttal after rebuttal to the plutocracy's propaganda.[37] They demonstrated that virtually no families were losing their farms due to this tax, and that only three-tenths of one percent of all estates were being taxed anything at all under the existing estate tax law.[38]

Fortunately, with the election of Barack Obama as president and a Democratic Congress in 2009 and 2010, the steam went out of the Republican drive to abolish the estate tax. Along the way, many Americans were educated about the estate tax. One of the best messages relayed through the media was an elevated foresight by Richard Rockefeller (of the legendary family): "If the world I leave behind is one of gated communities, growing inequality and misery among the have-nots, downward mobility for the middle class, a degraded environment and a rotting social and physical infrastructure—then [my children's] inheritance will be a shabby one—no matter how much money they get."[39]

FOUR

WHY DEMOCRACY WORKS

Let me state my thesis at the outset: It's a lot easier than you think to shape a political economy where corporations are our compliant servants, not our masters. When states like Massachusetts chartered corporations into existence during the early nineteenth century they did so by assigning them a subordinate position. At least that was the early ideal. The tables slowly turned to where we find ourselves today. The accumulation of profit allowed corporate elites to insinuate their influence over democracy and its non-market political institutions. Undermined as it has been by decades of deregulation and privatization, democracy still exists in the United States, and its participatory and egalitarian mechanisms for civil rights, social change, and justice remain our best tools to confront the power structure and change it. "We've found through our experience that timid supplications for justice will not solve the problem," said Martin Luther King Jr. in 1967 as he marshaled the civil rights movement's success toward larger national goals. "We've got to massively confront the power structure."[40]

It is also easier than you think to have elections where voters shape the agenda, where voters drive the candidates, where voters do the counting in competitive elections, and where using money to buy, rent, or influence politicians is banned. It's in our hands as voters if we want this kind of democracy.

The citizen muscle it will take to engender these transformations will likely awaken and unleash democratic forces to make Americans more economically and socially secure. It will also help the people to better harmonize the nation with the Earth's biosphere upon which all living things depend.

The following snapshots will shake up the pitiful worldview of those who have let themselves be convinced by the commercial culture that "it can't be done." It can be done! We don't have to live within corporate-imposed limitations. There is a better future around the corner if we work toward it together. So let us start with raising expectation levels—the ignition switch for change.

• • •

I'm staring with utter disbelief at the colorful cover of the July 20, 2014, edition of *Parade Magazine*, a publication inserted in your Sunday newspapers that has a circulation of millions. There staring back at me is a cat, named Mulligan from Minneapolis. This major feature article is about whether dogs dream or if cats can catch cold. Inside, I am afflicted with envy. Sockington, a cat rescued from a Boston subway, has 1.3 million Twitter followers. That's right, 1.3 million![41] I don't recall any *Parade* covers featuring people who save children's lives here or in developing countries. One such person was James Grant, a lawyer by profession, who headed UNICEF and personally persuaded dictators all over the world to follow measures for disease prevention or food distribution in order to save young children's lives. Then there are Patrick Burns, a prime corporate crime hunter; Bill Drayton, who has found and nurtured thousands of community leaders from three continents, who made local and national change; the law professors Barry Scheck and Peter Neufeld, and their students, who started the Innocence Project to exonerate innocent prisoners; Edgar and Jean Cahn, who pressured Congress to create the Legal Services Corporation that opened the pathways to legal representation for impoverished people; economist Jamie Love who, with his colleagues, broke Big Pharma's $10,000 per-patient price for a one-year prescription of medicine to treat AIDS by persuading an Indian drug company to provide the medication for $300 per patient, per year. Or Madeline Janis, head of Jobs to Move America, bringing jobs back to unionized workers. Never heard of them? They're just a few of many leaders changing or saving millions of people's lives. And their work is probably more exciting than celebrity cats and dogs, but you're not ever likely to read about them in the pages of *Parade* or magazines like it.

There was a time when *Parade* had a different, more serious mix of articles. About thirty years ago, for example, *Parade* had a feature on Ralf Hotchkiss, a former colleague, who revolutionized wheelchair manufacturing, breaking a true global wheel chair monopoly, by designing better, lighter, cheaper, and more durable wheelchairs that could be built from local materials in developing countries. But like most non-fiction periodicals, including the formerly august *New York Times Sunday Magazine* and the widely read *AARP Magazine*, the fare has become lighter and more superficial with every decade. The editors are reacting to what they are helping to create—a long slide down the ladder from substance and depth to celebrity and shallowness. As Phil Donahue once said to me, "We are a culture in decay." *Parade* has stories about the rich and famous, stories about athletes, advice about pets, remedies for personal anxieties, narratives of dramatic rescues, curiosa, factoids, recipes, quiz questions and the like, amidst medical and home alarm advertisements. As for *AARP Magazine*, stories about people in their seventies, eighties, and nineties accomplishing breakthrough endeavors never seem to make the cover page or even appear. We are permitting the mass media to diminish our expectation levels without pressuring them with our feedback.

This slide down the ladder of superficiality excludes an increasing number of serious articles that may not be as easy to take in, but are a prerequisite for a democracy-centered society that seeks to improve the harsh social realities that many Americans live with on a daily basis. We need to champion those remarkable people who are bringing us a better society. Their lives provide invaluable motivational role models for our children and communities. There is always a time for entertainment that requires light reading and short attention spans. But such material now seems to blanket the waterfront, and mobile devices seem to increase the availability of trivial content and violent games that compete for the bottom rung of mindlessness. Burdened by work and worries, it seems that an increasing number of people seek relaxation time where they can just be spectators of celebrity lifestyles, scandals, crime, and sports.

However, as the profane torrent of commercialized violence and fantasy claim more and more time and consciousness of adults and children, we find ourselves at the tipping point where we are less an engaged democracy and more a society of spectators. As the nation drifts toward authoritarianism, intolerance, and fear, we begin to resemble the societies described in George Orwell's *1984*, Aldous Huxley's *Brave New World*, and Todd Gitlin's *Entertaining Ourselves to Death*.

Perhaps sensing the intensification of a passive, entertainment-entranced culture, one of the world's foremost neuroscientists, Antonio R. Damasio, near the end of his acclaimed work *Descartes' Error*, offered this warning in 1994:

> Pain and pleasure are not twins or mirror images of each other, at least not as far as their roles in leveraging survival. Somehow, more often than not, it is the pain-related signal that steers us away from impending trouble, both at the moment and in the anticipated future. It is difficult to imagine that individuals and societies governed by the seeking of pleasure, as much or more than by the avoidance of pain, can survive at all.

So what would be required for society to break through power to pursue long overdue changes? It is a lot easier than we think. A lot easier than raising children, taking care of aging relatives, or trying to make ends meet. It requires less time and money than any one of a hundred popular hobbies in America. The first leveraging step is taken when one percent of the people connect with one another in legislative districts throughout the country, with each person devoting 300 volunteer hours a year and each raising two-hundred dollars to three-hundred dollars to staff full-time activist offices. The second step is taken in the form of the agenda citizens pursue through 535 members of Congress, and the support of public opinion—sixty to seventy percent—garnered through the force of creative social networking. Such public support is already out there, while many people are ready for the outreach necessary to reach those levels.

One percent of the country represents about 2.5 million adults (out of 250 million). Motivated by a diverse range of interconnected issues, these Americans will be bubbling over with moral indignation, passion, and commitment, as are those who give their time to advance the Black Lives Matter movement, the Climate Justice Movement, the Gun Control Movement, and Economic Justice Movement. Like the citizens of Flint, Michigan, who were mocked and dismissed for complaining that their water was poisoned, these ordinary Americans will be armed with personal stories of neglect, violence, and tragedy.[42] Like members of communities of color who organize against police violence in their neighborhoods, engaged citizens will come with their neighbors, their families, and an uncompromising love that cannot be bought. These Americans, guided by conscience, will demand more meaning of life, and have a deep understanding about what it takes to have a functioning democracy that genuinely serves the needs and meets the aspirations of our communities.

Gaining the critical backing of the "public sentiment" is easier than we think. Regardless of all the reports from Rush Limbaugh and FOX News that the United States is a highly polarized society, there are already, as we shall review, many important areas of social and political convergence in the United States. Ruling classes throughout history have always used divide-and-conquer strategies that deliberately undermine organic solidarities between advocates focused on specific issues and across lines of race, gender, and class.

Consider major changes in U.S. history. Was there ever more than one percent of the American population actively pressing for abolition of slavery prior to the Civil War, for guaranteeing women the right to vote, or for advancing the right of workers to organize unions? Very unlikely. Year after year a small number of engaged Americans still exert enormous influence in changing public opinion in favor of breaking through power for greater freedom, justice, and democracy for all.

The same was true for the farmers' populist revolts of the late nineteenth century that led to historic progressive reforms, as well as those social movements that fought for increased regulation of Big Business, fair labor standards, the abolition of child labor, Social Security, Medicare, and civil rights. Far less than one percent increased "public sentiment" to force Congress and the White House to enact major consumer, worker safety, and environmental protections into law during the 1960s and 1970s.

In the 1960s, when some of us in Washington began taking on the mighty cigarette industry, it was considered nearly impossible to loosen the tobacco barons' well-financed grip on Congress. Our strategy was to hit their weakest points by pushing for no-smoking sections on airplanes, interstate trains, and buses and for Fairness Doctrine time so that anti-cigarette ads could appear on nationwide television stations. Our strategy worked.

One intrepid, smart law professor, John Banzhaf, of George Washington University Law School, played a very important role in the demand to prevent tobacco companies from advertising on television. The impact of the historic U.S. Surgeon General's first report on tobacco and health in 1964 hit like a wrecking ball. By forcefully connecting smoking with lung cancer, public opinion rose up against the corporations that profited from addiction to their product.

In 1964, about 45 percent of all adults were smoking regularly. That still left a majority of non-smokers, who began to receive support for the separation of smokers from non-smokers and their children in trains, planes, and buses. In 1967 Professor Banzhaf founded Action on Smoking and Health (ASH), a national non-profit legal action and educational organization that successfully fought for the rights of non-smokers. In 1972 the U.S. Supreme Court agreed with the arguments made in ASH's brief and affirmed that the law banning cigarette commercials is constitutional. Non-smokers became a more demanding constituency, often led by people whose families were afflicted with asthma, emphysema, cancer, and tobacco addiction. Those advocating smoke-free areas began to receive public attention. Fearing the impact of caustic counter-ads, the industry dropped their television ads in 1969.

You can see the elements that were converging at the

time—medical research about tobacco-related deaths, a few dozen full-time advocates to foster media reporting, assertive non-smokers, physicians advising their patients not to smoke, the warning labels on cigarette packs and in print ads, and ever-decreasing public space available for smokers. These actions laid the groundwork for "stage two" in the 1980s when tort litigation, industry whistleblowers, exposés in major newspapers and national media like *60 Minutes*, followed by hitherto unheard of Congressional hearings, started breaking through the power of the tobacco business and their lobbyists on Capitol Hill. With each year of organizing, the price of cigarettes was driven up, the amount of public spaces available to smoke was driven down, and the number of people buying the addictive product continued to shrink. The public's "anti-tobacco fervor," to quote a phrase from the *New York Times*, continued to intensify. Today less than twenty percent of Americans smoke cigarettes. Along the way, top executives of the largest American tobacco companies lied as long as they could, suppressed research, and as late as 1994 "testified in Congress that they did not believe that cigarettes were addictive."[43]

In 2009 Congress acted independently of corporate influence and passed legislation giving the Food and Drug Administration regulatory authority over the tobacco industry. With anti-tobacco sentiment reaching a state of fervor amoung the public, the taboos on taking on the tobacco industry were lifted. Most members of Congress felt they could start standing up to this industry.

The mass destruction caused by tobacco is thousands of times greater than the threat to national security that is posed by ISIS, Al Qaeda, or the Taliban. Each year, the tobacco business costs Americans tens of billions of dollars in healthcare costs, lost productivity, fires, and over 400,000 deaths. What has it taken to break through the power of the cigarette business? There has been, to my knowledge, no thorough estimate of the time and money invested in national defense against this sickening industry. However, long-standing opponent of Big Tobacco, Michael Pertschuk, former Chief of Staff to the Senate Commerce Committee and Chairman of the Federal Trade Commission, provided me with his ballpark estimate. At its peak in the mid-1980s, the movement against cigarettes and tobacco, he said, comprised no more than a few thousand full-time researchers and advocates backed by grants from the American Cancer Society, the American Lung Association, and assorted donations from the public. By partial contrast, the tobacco companies paid just one law firm, Arnold & Porter, $10 million each year to run the Tobacco Institute. Even as Big Tobacco—chiefly Phillip Morris, Reynolds Tobacco, and Lorillard—was assuming a defensive posture and losing its influence, billions of dollars were still being spent on tobacco promotion while tens of thousands of people were on the payroll working full-time to protect and advance profiteering from tobacco.

Despite this war chest and nicotine's promotional army, Big Tobacco is still losing ground in the United States on all fronts, including sales. To make up for some of this decline, this greed-driven industry is moving into the electronic cigarette business and stepping up its nefarious politicking for large markets in developing countries with the insidious muscle of the U.S. Chamber of Commerce.[44] Enough is now known about rolling back tobacco to have Western governments, together with the World Health Organization, and some philanthropists like former New York City mayor Michael Bloomberg, formidably raise the ante in the global attack on cigarette sales and addiction. Given the many millions of lives that can be saved from addiction, disease, and death, what is required in money and manpower is well worth the cost and effort.

What may be considered an impossible dream—slowing down and diminishing the nuclear weapons arms race between Washington and Moscow—began touching reality under the Reagan administration. When Ronald Reagan started seeing tens of thousands of Americans marching in the streets of Washington D.C. and New York City to show support for a nuclear weapons reduction treaty, he noticed there were some well-dressed Republicans in their midst. Polls showed support for arms control treaties. Members of the military—active and retired—saw the futility of spending tax dollars on mutually assured destruction that they saw as having no strategic value. The former head of the Strategic Air Command, retired General George Lee Butler, began speaking out about the importance of arms control all over the country and got media coverage.[45] Citizen groups such as Nuclear Freeze Coalition, led by New Englanders Randall Forsberg and Randy Keeler, who said "enough is enough" to the thousands of stockpiled nuclear bombs and missiles, mobilized the grassroots. Michael Deaver, President Reagan's closest advisor, acknowledged that the Nuclear Freeze movement influenced White House Policy.[46]

By the time Reagan met with Mikhail Gorbachev, the head of the U.S.S.R., in Reykjavik, Iceland, it was Mr. Republican who blurted out to Gorby that they should get rid of all nuclear weapons. His Russian counterpart agreed.[47] Nothing that far-reaching made it to paper, but it did lead to accords between the two super-powers for exchanging inspectors to check the dismantling of nuclear warheads to less than one-third of the total that existed at the peak. Behind the scenes, a number of enormously important, little celebrated, civil servants worked on the sticky details in these accords, such as lawyer Thomas Graham, a skillful federal arms control negotiator.[48]

To free the United States—and the world—from nuclear weapons, much still remains to be done, of course. But a few dozen determined and knowledgeable people from military and civilian backgrounds, plus a few dozen organizers of mass marches, rallies, and demonstrations, and a few dozen prominent scholars, writers, musicians, and artists who developed an anti-nuke culture, helped fuel the rise in "public sentiment" that impacted policy. The fight to stop the proliferation, manufacturing, and hoarding of nuclear weapons, like efforts to end slavery or prevent the negative impacts of climate change, depends entirely on people's actions, which can turn the tide toward a just and sustainable future. Unfortunately, the pursuit of limitless profits stands in the way of justice, reason, and, some might argue, sanity.

As if one set of corporations dedicated to addicting youngsters to a lethal drug and another set pushing Congress for endless weapons of mass destruction were not enough, consider the "get Americans fatter" fast-food companies all over the USA. McDonald's, Burger King, Wendy's and other fast-fooders learned long ago that it pays off to serve larger portions of food, loaded with fat, sugar, and salt, coupled with larger, heavily-sweetened soft drinks. By hooking youngsters at an early age with direct advertising that undermines parental authority, this industry made its marketing objectives crystal clear. The earlier in life a person learned to like processed food, the better. The more corpulent the customer, the larger their desire to consume processed food and sugared drink products. As outside studies poured into their executive suites on rising obesity (68.8 percent are considered to be overweight or obese, 35.7 percent are considered to be obese)[49] and their associated costly illnesses—diabetes, high blood pressure, clogged arteries at early ages, orthopedic replacements of knees and hips, to name a few—the big junk food executives profitably looked the other way, just like the executives of big tobacco did.

Sometime around 1970 I visited the Massachusetts Institute of Technology to interview students for our work. One of them was a graduating microbiology PhD student named Michael Jacobson. He joined us in Washington and in 1971 launched, with two other of our young scientists, Dr. Al Fritsch and Dr. James Sullivan, the Center for Science in the Public Interest (CSPI), a non-profit organization dedicated to transforming the American diet through strong advocacy for "nutrition and health, food safety, alcohol policy, and sound science." Dr. Jacobson is still making history, still breaking through the power of the food giants, the Food and Drug Administration, and the U.S. Department of Agriculture with widely publicized reports, a mass-circulation newsletter, *Nutrition Action*, Congressional testimony, litigation, and interviews in A-list national media. Of course he has a staff dedicated to equating food with health and nutrition in the minds of consumers and translating that into pressure on food companies, restaurants, and regulators. CSPI's staff is smaller than a small town's Rotary Club. But when you steadily put forces in motion that embody what people believe is good for themselves and their children, the leverage of a few for the benefit of the many is often enormous.

Newton Minow's broad evaluation of American television as "a vast wasteland" did not startle Everett C. Parker, who already was planning his one-man attack on the broadcasting industry's exclusion of people of color and dissenting viewpoints. Mr. Parker was an ordained minister. After graduating from the University of Chicago, he worked as a radio producer in Chicago and New Orleans and later started up an advertising agency in the windy city before entering the Chicago Theological Seminary. While teaching at the Yale Divinity School from 1945 to 1957, he delved deeply into broadcasting projects. He took seriously the neglected 1934 Communications Act that required licensed radio stations (later television stations) to adhere to the standard of the "public interest, convenience or necessity." To Dr. Parker that meant stations were obliged to assess the information needs of the local communities that received the broadcasts, providing more than one side of issues of public significance (the Fairness Doctrine issued by the FCC) and offering equal time on controversial issues of public importance and the right of reply when individuals or groups were sharply denounced or slandered.

Everett Parker was a quiet dynamo who put many forces into motion for media reform of the television and radio industries. In a singular breakthrough, in 1964, he challenged the broadcast license renewal of WLBT TV in Jackson, Mississippi, for egregious bigotry in its coverage of the Civil Rights Movement. Challenges to license renewals at that time were only filed by other broadcasters and were rare. Licenses were automatically renewed by the industry-indentured FCC.

As the Director of the Office of Communications of the United Church of Christ, Dr. Parker decided to sue the FCC, except he could not find an attorney in Washington who would take the case. He eventually found a young lawyer in New York, Early K. Moore, who would stick with him for his entire career, and he took the FCC to court and won a resounding, groundbreaking decision by federal appellate court rescinding WLBT's license in 1969. In an opinion written by conservative Judge Warren E. Burger, who became Chief of Justice of the U.S. Supreme Court, the appeals court ruled that "after nearly five decades of operation, the broadcast industry does not seem to have grasped the simple fact that a broadcast license is a public trust subject to termination for breach of duty."

Branching out and recruiting people all over the country, some of whom established full-time reform groups, Dr. Parker aroused a sizable sector of the public to realize that the public airwaves belong to the people and that there should be serious consequences for radio and television broadcasters who violate the public interest mandate. On the occasion of his passing at the age of one hundred and two in

September, 2015, the *New York Times* recounted his efforts in the 1970s to organize education and internship programs for minority students interested in broadcasting. The *Times* quoted Dr. Parker, who in 1967 declared that "discriminating practices by some Southern stations is a continuing daily insult to the Negro people these stations are licensed to serve. Such discrimination is an affront to Americans everywhere who grant exclusive licenses to broadcasters only to see some of them openly defy the laws of the land."[50]

The "public sentiment" that Everett Parker helped to galvanize inspired members of the Federal Communications Commission, such as Commissioner Nicolas Johnson, to advance these reforms and further educate the public. Having been involved in bolstering the Fairness Doctrine and the Right of Reply, since rescinded, along with the need for better local and national programming, I came across the endeavors and ripples of Dr. Parker's work throughout the country. The reforms which his leadership created were sustained and some have survived the assaults on regulation of the Reagan era and beyond. Dr. Everett C. Parker demonstrates how one person can make a difference. One lesson from his valiant efforts is that all reforms will suffer counterattacks if they do not produce expanding, institutional defenses in the public sphere. This has not occured, unfortunately. It takes just a few thousand people to achieve some degree of media accountability on behalf of the tens of millions of people who are regularly exposed to programming—overwhelmingly corporate entertainment and advertising—driven by profit-seeking, not the public trust required by under-enforced federal law.

A small community—probably less than two dozen people over the past fifty years—has won many improvements in the passenger airline industry. A project led by two Princeton engineering students in the late 1960s on the low level of safety standards for small general aviation planes—which were not even required to have seat belts—led to the enactment of safer standards. Then my lawsuit against Allegheny Airlines for overbooking and bumping me despite a confirmed reservation won a unanimous U.S. Supreme Court decision. The case, brilliantly argued by public interest lawyer Reuben Robertson, permanently changed the way airlines treat over-booked passengers with reservations. Today airline staff either have to ask if any seated passengers want to give up their seats, receive compensation, and take the next flight out, or the airlines have to compensate the bumped passengers, usually from $650 to $1,300. Day after day, all over the country, the effects of this decision work like a charm.

About the same time, in 1972, I started the Aviation Consumer Action Project (ACAP) that gave several activist staff the opportunity to show what a tiny number of advocates can do for tens of millions of airline passengers and flight attendants. With the media avidly reporting ACAP proposals, the airlines were pressured to eliminate smoking sections, to make higher payments for lost baggage, to more fully disclose charges and fees on tickets, to provide emergency medical kits and to ban post-purchase price-fare increases. Pressure from these and a few other safety advocates, such as Paul Hudson, has produced or accelerated improved safety and security standards and internal enhancements to reduce air-traffic delay congestion, and to protect passengers during crashes. While airlines certainly have their own incentives for advancing safety, their poor labor policies, restrictive consumer services, and frequent exemption from state and local consumer laws often bring the worst out in them, requiring constant consumer vigilance.

Kate Hanni saw this firsthand one day when she and other passengers on a Delta flight were stranded on the Austin Airport tarmac for over nine hours in increasingly oppressive conditions. Angered into action, she started a consumer group called Flyersrights.org and soon, with good media coverage, had over twenty-five thousand members who sent this non-profit small contributions. Today Flyersrights.org is the largest non-profit consumer organization representing airline passengers. One of her many achievements was to require that passengers be given food and water and be allowed to deplane when aircraft have to remain on the tarmac for more than three hours on domestic flights and four hours on international flights.

One of the most uniquely astonishing individuals to have broken through power and the scourge of voicelessness was a Spanish immigrant named Concepcion Picciotto. Intensely committed to movements against war and nuclear weapons and for peace, she started a 24/7 protest in 1981 in front of the White House in an encampment on the edge of Lafayette Square. She called her effort a "Peace Park Anti-Nuclear Vigil"—probably the longest continual civic-political protest in U.S. history.

When she received the Joe A. Callaway Award for Civic Courage in 2011, the award citation described her with these words: "In recognition of her exceptional 30-year, day and night anti-nuclear peace vigil, her moral achievement affirming a belief in strength through peace, her physical endurance surviving snowstorms, hurricanes, sub-zero temperatures and summer heat; her strong survival capacities and resilience under physical and verbal abuse, 'the Little Giant' as she has been described, has set the highest standard for testing the authenticity of free speech protection under the Constitution."

Thanks to the champions of the First Amendment and a court decision, Concepcion's encampment withstood the National Park Service's readiness to shut her down if she and a few friends who supported her for a few hours daily did not occupy the site 24 hours a day without sleeping. Incredible! Imagine her stamina!

She had signs presenting President Eisenhower's warnings about the military-industrial complex, and buttons championing the oppressed of the Earth; she gave out pamphlets and donated books to some of the millions of people who passed by, mostly tourists from all over the country and the world. She was written about by media worldwide: the *Northern Ireland Times* called her location a moral "Maginot Line" and its occupants "Watchers at the Gate," a daily reminder to presidents (none of whom have ever visited her) that nuclear weapons of mass destruction are the ultimate madness.[51] Barely able to pay her one-room rental, this humble woman and nearly penniless protestor answered questions as to why she kept holding her vigil year after year: "for the children," who must be taught to "respect and value LIFE, not material things." Knowing that her message is supported by much of humanity but ignored by mainstream media, she created her own daily media in the most politically magnetic place in the world: in front of the White House. Concepcion passed away in a homeless shelter for women on January 25, 2016, passing the torch of her spirit and determination to us to carry forward. "Through her presence," reported the *Washington Post* in their honorary obituary, "she said she hoped to remind others to take whatever action they could, however small, to help end wars and stop violence, particularly against children."[52]

"Why should I listen to anything Harry Kelber says?" exclaimed a visibly indignant Richard Trumka, president of the AFL-CIO, in a meeting with us in his book-lined office. Well, one response is that for nearly 80 years, this consummate union worker, organizer, advocate, and pamphleteer has been right about the causes behind the stagnation and decline of the organized labor movement. That has meant steady criticism by him of the AFL-CIO and other unions, large and small. Secrecy, corruption, self-enrichment, failure to spend on union organizing, and top-down autocratic leadership are some of Kelber's soft-spoken but relentless critiques. Right up to his last days at age 98, Kelber, working out of his modest Brooklyn apartment, poured forth his thoughts in regular columns on his blog, laboreducator.org. Over the decades, his pamphlets, so clearly written, were circulated in the millions. Among his "bestsellers" were "The Making of Ideal Union Leaders," "The Making of Ideal Union Members," "Why Unions Are in Politics," "Why Unions Are Good for You and Your Family" (also in Spanish), and "A Training Manual for Union Organizers."

Harry Kelber spoke and wrote about what is on the minds of millions of union and non-union workers. Why aren't organized labor's leaders more aggressive in addressing the plight of America's labor by challenging big companies and their political allies? Specifically, he asked, why didn't the AFL-CIO leadership hold Barack Obama accountable for his 2008 promises to press Congress for a $9.50 federal minimum wage?[53] Why didn't Obama, when Congress was under full control of the Democrats in 2009–2010, press Congress to pass the "card check" legislation he promised? Card check rights, Mr. Trumka told me in 2004, is all he would need to organize workers into unions in places like Walmart and McDonald's. Many Democrats can't get elected without union support, but once they win office most invariably turn their backs on workers' needs to have their pensions protected; turn their backs on confronting corporate globalization, on preventing the outsourcing of jobs to repressive dictatorships abroad, and even on attempts to repeal horrendous anti-worker laws such as the notorious Taft-Hartley Act of 1947.

Harry Kelber, in his eighties, went into the lions' den as a lone-wolf candidate when he challenged the incumbent president of the AFL-CIO. He never had a chance at winning the election, of course, given how the rules were rigged. But one rule allowed any candidate to address the large convention of union delegates who are the electors. Standing before them, Kelber delivered an impassioned, fact-filled, anti-incumbent speech before the assemblage of delegates who totally supported the incumbent president. Nonetheless, they gave the veteran union champion a standing ovation. Maybe they thought that Kelber had something to teach them, unlike the opinion voiced in Richard Trumka's outburst.

When Kelber was in his nineties he gave up on the AFL-CIO and the large salaries and benefits of union chiefs. He urged the creation of a new federation of workers that would place a high priority on the unionization of tens of millions of low-paid workers, who, polls showed, would like to join a union.

Although I had known about scientists' concern about climate change back in the 1980s, it was the dramatic report, *The Climate Change Action Plan*, signed by President William J. Clinton and Vice President Albert Gore Jr. in October, 1993, that really caught my attention. President Clinton used urgent language to present his extraordinarily-detailed *Climate Change Action Plan* that is almost as fresh today as the day it was written. Six months earlier, in April 1993, President Clinton issued "a clarion call" for rapid implementation, adding, "We must take the lead in addressing the challenge of global warming that could make our planet and its climate less hospitable and more hostile to human life."[54] (I took this report, still at my desk, seriously throughout my campaigns.) So what did Mr. Clinton proceed to do? He gave the auto industry *carte blanche* for eight years. Instead of increasing fuel efficiency standards, he subsidized the auto industry with over a billion dollars to research and develop a low-emission motor vehicle. Taxpayers got nothing from that "public/private partnership." Clinton proceeded to expand leasing for oil, gas, and coal, and kept Al Gore, author of the 1992 book *Earth in the Balance*, muzzled from touting vigorous productive expansion of solar energy, other renewables, and technological efficiencies.

None of these anomalies escaped the attention of a young writer, Bill McKibben, who by 1989 had already written *The End of Nature*, an urgent book about global warming. Ten years ago, while holding a distinguished scholar position at Middlebury College, he and his students decided that more action was needed. And so 350.org was born, arguably the big oil, gas, and coal companies' biggest nightmare.

I called McKibben and asked him to tell the story in his own words:

> 350.org grew out of a march some of us organized across Vermont in 2006. After five days of walking, we had 1,000 people gather in Burlington. That was a good crowd for Vermont, but the stories in the paper said it may have been the largest climate demonstration that had yet taken place in America. We knew, all of a sudden, why we were losing. We had the infrastructure of a movement—the scientists, the policy people, and so on. We just didn't have the movement part. We thought there should be mass organizing around this greatest of issues.
>
> So seven students at Middlebury and myself went to work. First we did a one-day series of events, in the spring of 2007, across America. We called it StepItUp, and organized 1,400 rallies in all 50 states. It proved to us that the Internet allowed for the organization of widely distributed simultaneous events, and so in 2008 we took the model

global with 350.org. In our first big day of action, we helped coordinate 5,200 events in 181 countries, which CNN called "the most widespread day of political activity in the planet's history." We didn't "organize" them—no one can organize on that vast a scale. It was more like throwing a potluck dinner—we set the date and the theme, and then people pitched in, mostly across the developing world. And over the next couple of years the party grew steadily larger—by some estimates we've coordinated 20,000 rallies in every country but North Korea.

If we had a few decades to solve global warming, we'd just keep going on this kind of "education by activism." But given the fast-deteriorating climate, we've had to turn education into confrontation quickly. Hence, for instance, the fight against Keystone, with many allies especially among indigenous communities. It won—but its more important victory was spawning a thousand similar fights, what one fossil fuel exec called the "Keystonization" of projects around the world. Or the divestment campaign, which has pulled trillions of dollars' worth of endowments out of fossil fuel—but more importantly driven home the argument that we have five times as much fossil fuel in our reserves as we can burn. In essence, it's turning the fossil fuel giants into rogue companies.

I've never been the leader of this organization (or this movement), just a committed and engaged

> volunteer. 350.org is run by May Boeve, one of those original Middlebury students, and it's now grown to have about a hundred staff around the world, most of them young people. That seems enormous to me—but, given the scale of the challenge, I guess it's not really.

Pretty modest reflections for one of the best-known advocates in the world. But then again, McKibben understands that a central goal of movement leadership is to create more leaders, not more followers. That's how he achieved a first in U.S. history—leading a drive around the White House in 2011 where over 1,200 people, protesting the XL Keystone Pipeline, were arrested in one of the largest acts of nonviolent mass civil disobedience.

As for one person's capacity for breaking through power, far too many people think it's too difficult to be done, and thus they sell themselves far too short. A wave of pessimism leads capable people to underestimate the power of their voice and the strength of their ideals. The evidential truth is this: it is the initiatives of deeply caring regular people that provide the firmament for our democracy.

Take a sweeping look at history and you will discover that almost all movements that mattered started with just one or two people—from the fight to abolish slavery, to the creations of the environmental, trade union, consumer protection and civil rights movements. One voice becomes two, and then ten, and then thousands.

The year 2017 will mark the 80th anniversary of the sit-down strike in Flint, Michigan, where thousands of powerless and frustrated workers sat down in a General Motors factory to fight for recognition of the newly formed United Auto Workers (UAW) union. On February 11, 1937, General Motors conceded. The giant company raised wages and labor standards and recognized the UAW, a major win for unionization in the United States.[55] This is an aspect of the American story that most people love and celebrate, yet are quick to dismiss as being improbable in today's partisan, corporate-dominated world. But, as I often say, real change is easier than you think. As Marge Piercy says in her movement poem "The Low Road":

> It goes on one at a time,
> it starts when you care
> to act, it starts when you do
> it again and they said no,
> it starts when you say *We*
> and know who you mean, and each
> day you mean one more.[56]

Howard Zinn said: "Small acts, when multiplied by millions of people, can quietly become a power no government can suppress, a power that can transform the world."[57]

The following twelve men and women maximized their power as citizens to improve the lives of millions of people in real, tangible ways. May their stories inspire millions more, so as to become a power no government can suppress, a power that can transform the world.

LOIS GIBBS

Lois Gibbs was raising her family in the Love Canal neighborhood of Niagara Falls, New York, when news of the toxic contamination beneath her feet made local headlines. Starting with no political or economic power whatsoever, Lois organized her neighbors into what was known as the Love Canal Homeowners Association. Her movement grew to become the country's largest grassroots anti-corporate contamination movement. She later founded the Center for Health, Environment & Justice, which has worked with ten thousand local groups to battle toxic dangers in their neighborhoods and win many of these struggles.

RALF HOTCHKISS

I first met Ralf over 40 years ago at Oberlin College where he was majoring in physics and moving about the campus in a wheelchair after a motorcycle accident had rendered him paraplegic. Recognizing a need for low-cost, sustainable, and versatile wheelchairs, he started Whirlwind Wheelchair to teach people around the world how to manufacture their own affordable, sturdier wheelchairs, which he helped invent, in small shop facilities using local materials. Along the way as noted earlier he was a leader in breaking the London-based wheelchair monopoly by helping new manufacturers get their products to market.

CLARENCE DITLOW

Once described by *The New York Times* as "the splinter the [auto] industry cannot remove from its thumb," Clarence Ditlow is an engineer, lawyer, and Executive Director of the Center for Auto Safety. He has been responsible for car companies initiating millions of lifesaving recalls, and was instrumental in the passage of "lemon laws" in all 50 states, which make sure consumers receive reparations for defective automobiles.

AL FRITSCH

A Jesuit priest and Ph.D, Al Fritsch was the environmental consultant 45 years ago at our Center for the Study of Responsive Law in Washington D.C. before returning to his roots in Appalachia to start the Appalachia Center for Science in the Public Interest. Using applied science and technology, Al Fritsch is a driving force for locally-based sustainability and maintaining a healthy planet.

RAY ANDERSON

The late Ray Anderson was founder and CEO of Interface, the world's largest modular carpet manufacturing firm based in Atlanta, Georgia. Disturbed by the hugely damaging effects of industry on the environment, he shifted his company's directive to "make peace with the planet." With the ultimate goal of zero pollution and 100 percent recycling for his company, he managed to move significantly toward these objectives while reducing expenses and increasing profits year after year. Why aren't more CEOs following his example?

ANNIE LEONARD

With her widely successful Story of Stuff Project, Annie Leonard scoured the world for the stories that tell the tale of where our throwaway economy is leading us (hint: it doesn't have a happy ending). Her imaginative 20-minute *Story of Stuff* film has been watched and shared online by millions, and was turned into a book and an ongoing website. She is now the Executive Director of Greenpeace.

WENONAH HAUTER

As the founder and Director of Food & Water Watch, with its hundred full-time staff around the country, farmer Wenonah has fought tirelessly for the future of our food, water, energy, and environment. A relentless organizer, author, and activist, she is a champion of getting citizens involved in issues that matter most—the things we put in our bodies.

REVEREND DR. WILLIAM J. BARBER

The Rev. Dr. William Barber walks with a cane but, with thousands of collaborators, he is making big strides for justice and equality through his organizing of "Moral Mondays" protests, which first started in North Carolina. The protests started as a response to the "mean-spirited quadruple attack" on the most vulnerable members of our society. In the tradition of the Rev. Martin Luther King, Rev. Barber is fighting against restrictions on voting and for improvements in labor laws. In addition to his work as a minister, Rev. Barber is the President of the North Carolina chapter of the NAACP.

MICHAEL MARIOTTE

For over 30 years, Michael Mariotte has been a dynamic leader in successful movements against nuclear power in the United States. As the President of the Nuclear Information and Resource Service, Michael has testified before Congress and spoken in countries around the world against the catastrophic dangers of nuclear power and the unsolved problem of how to store highly radioactive "spent fuel rods" without causing irreparable damage to the natural environment.

DAVID HALPERIN

David is a tenacious advocate and tireless worker for justice who has launched several advocacy organizations and projects such as Progressive Networks, The American Constitution Society, and Campus Progress. Nothing gives him greater joy than thwarting those individuals in positions of power in our society who seek to profit from unjust practices. Most recently, Attorney Halperin has focused his considerable talents on exposing the predatory and deceptive practices of for-profit colleges.

SIDNEY WOLFE

Dr. Sidney M. Wolfe and I started the Public Citizen Health Research Group in 1971 to promote good healthcare policy and drug safety. Dr. Wolfe, through his *Worst Pills, Best Pills* books, newsletters, and outreach via the *Phil Donahue Show*, has exposed the brand names of hundreds of ineffective FDA-approved drugs, or effective drugs with harmful side effects, which were forced to be removed from the marketplace.

DOLORES HEURTA

A legendary activist, Dolores Heurta cofounded the United Farm Workers Union with Cesar Chavez in the 1960s and has a long history of fighting for social change, workers' rights, and civil justice. Unlike many other awardees, she was rightfully awarded the Presidential Medal of Freedom in 2011, among many other recognitions.

Our country has more problems than it should tolerate, and more solutions than it uses. Why should we continue to allow corporate culture to silence our voices? People matter, *you* matter, and systemic change will only happen when people, families, communities, and networks speak out, gather, and act together like a wrecking ball to break through the callous self-interest of plutocracy and cruel unjust power.

The many, many examples of people acting ethically and making a big difference are so threaded throughout American history that it is astonishing that our educational system doesn't make their examples a major part of in-class curricula from the first grade onward. Schools do not even use the books featuring stories of civic "heroes" written for different age groups to teach how truth can speak and discipline power. The stories of controversial founding fathers, military heroes, political leaders, and business pioneers, however, are taught to millions of students. Few students can join these ranks, but they all can aspire to becoming heroic citizens since democracy, like a public library, does not have any price of admission for participation at the local, state, or national levels. Everyone starts with citizen rights; and their education should stimulate them to aspire to various civic roles. Alas, as public and private education become more commercial in purpose, the teaching of civics, civic skills, and civic experience right in the community receives too little attention and is not promoted as an educational priority. This sad state reduces the number of youngsters who will learn how to become engaged citizens. Really, how difficult would it be to turn this around in communities nationwide?

Candidates for public office, especially at the local level, are sometimes too few to even provide the public with choices. Often, of the 2.5 million local elected positions in the United States—such as town councils, boards of education, and other commissions—many incumbents run without challengers. Voter turnout is very low. The political party machines accept the fact that people are withdrawn from voting and pursue commercialized sources of political contributions to which they become beholden, and thereby further consolidate the power of plutocracy. As this occurs, elections increasingly drift outside the arenas of a democratic society and become a spectacle that people tune in and out of, without being active participants in the political process.

So why do people drop out of the process? There are usually four explanations. The most common is: "I just don't have the time." If they do have time, the next reply is: "I don't know how to go about it and decipher that legal stuff at city council meetings or the rules they throw at us." If that is not the obstacle, the next stage is, "Well, I'm worried about my job or my promotion if the controversy rubs the boss the wrong way. Besides, I can't stand the slander and the bruising attacks on my character or integrity." If all these are surmounted, the final "excuse" is, "It won't make any difference anyway because the big boys always get their way." And this is the way many potentially effective citizens resign themselves to futility and do nothing.

Reaching out to the several million capable people who have allowed themselves to become inert is an important part of not just breaking through power, but in what comes after: sustaining democracy and strengthening a just society. Personally bonding with people at a community level is essential. Social networks drive social movements. Once people start getting involved, they no longer feel that they are frozen in amber. Like most endeavors in life, from occupations to hobbies, training and preparation pave the way for confident performance. Imagine just overcoming the challenges to be good at the game of bridge or poker, or learning a second language or sustainable gardening. Training and preparation! Civic knowhow includes using the freedom of information laws to get material from the federal and state governments, learning how to build coalitions, organize demonstrations, generate media coverage, share credit, and become resilient to overcome the expected mistakes and losses. It means community building.

Breaking through power to build and sustain a just democracy will require that the one or so percent of the people who are already community-minded reach out to mobilize other sectors of society. This one percent requires volunteers for fund-raising drives, elections, various town or neighborhood meetings, petition drives, and forums on controversial causes. What motivates this one percent of the nation to spend say 300 hours a year on such initiatives? I call it a "civic personality," one that is inspired by a sense of community, purpose, self-respect, and a search for a more meaningful experience of life. A friend once asked my mother how she could spend so much time on community activities when she had a family with four children to take care of every day. She replied: "That's part of taking care of family. Isn't the health of our community good for raising a family? They go together." I have never forgotten her words.

Taking the needs of community personally is a sign of social commitment. It is a form of self-respect that refuses to firewall public duties from private life. We need to cultivate this sensibility across lines of age, race, class, gender, and political orientation. How? Well, not surprisingly it starts with parents and upbringing. Whenever I ask seasoned activists and leaders how they got into these activities and persisted, one frequent response is that their parents took them, as children, to rallies, marches, demonstrations, public meetings, and courtrooms. That's what may be called the "hereditary factor." Encouraged to observe and make comments afterwards, the youngsters asked their parents questions about the events. These are parents who converse with their children, regularly read to them, and give them enough space to forge their capacity to turn their backs on the pack (their peers) and develop a more independent, less conforming personality. I am sure you can fill in the blanks regarding all the other ways to encourage children to value community and to grow up participating in local collaborations.

Another deep source of motivation for activism is preventable tragedy. Personal calamities such as the killing of unarmed people of color on streets all over the country has directly led to the national Black Lives Matter movement. Those killed by drunk drivers directly led to Candy Lightner's creation of Mothers Against Drunk Driving. Those who have been unable to prevent greedy bankers from unjustly seizing their homes have driven a national anti-foreclosure movement. Those who survive violence—particularly abuse by institutions and authorities—fervently desire to protect others from the people, power, and policies that have harmed them and their families. Many a safety regulation has emerged from activists who target the perpetrators of unsafe products. These activists produce testimony, and create conditions for accountability and progressive change.

There is an infrequently used incentive that could help people overcome the feeling that they are greatly outnumbered by opposing interests: asking people to pledge to act or donate only if a certain number of additional people would also pledge a similar amount of effort. Consider a pledge program if you and your community are trying to establish a local Congress Watch Project in your Congressional District, and you want 1,000 people to raise $200 a year each for a full-time staff and also to volunteer 300 hours a year—all to assure that your congressional representatives adopt and press for your agenda in Congress. Signing people up one at a time is a challenge. Some potential supporters might not have confidence that the objective can be met. But if you say to people, you don't have to give and volunteer unless we get 999 other people making the same pledge, there will probably be more of a buy-in.

Another sizeable portion of our population, lacking the social safety net that Western Europeans and Canadians grant themselves, spend large amounts of their time caring for ailing members of their extended family. There is very little paid family-leave time (not to mention paid maternity leave) in the land of the free, home of the brave. With lower average hourly pay and less social insurance than in our Western counterparts, many people have to balance two jobs and care for ailing relatives and friends in a 24-hour day.

The October/November 2015 issue of *AARP Magazine* published a feature article, with poignant pictures, titled "A Day in the Life of the American Caregiver." Some telling facts were recounted: "In the United States, about forty million people provide unpaid care to an ill or disabled adult. One-quarter of these caregivers have been in their roles for five years or longer." Each page pairs touching pictures of their daily care with a description of the disability and how the caregiver teaches us "the meaning of devotion." Add up the number of people giving and receiving care, and the total is approximately 100 million people. Where is the time for these people to be engaged in breaking through power?

Perhaps there are another thirty or forty million adults who are pure homebodies, whether through extreme privacy, shyness, anxiety, a sense of self-sufficiency, or just plain not wanting to be bothered. We all know people who prefer to "keep to themselves"; other humans are not their concern.

The overall point here is that many people are in positions where they cannot see themselves participating in a democratic society beyond paying their taxes, observing the laws, and just trying to make ends meet. If you add the people with serious diseases such as debilitating cancer, arthritis, hepatitis C, or advanced diabetes, additional millions of people have understandable medical challenges that limit their capacity for civic action.

Despite this, some of the most determined and amazing change-agents have been seriously disabled, including, of course, those citizens who pioneered and led the revolutionary movement for equal access and equal opportunity for Americans with disabilities. Moreover, some of those who have such compelling reasons for staying outside the civic arena can greatly help build the "public sentiment" that Lincoln so valued. Making phone calls to legislators, urging friends to attend public meetings, or responding to calls from public opinion surveyors are among many simple things that take a few minutes and enliven a hard-pressed routine.

Changes for a better society often start with the power structures sensing a growing rumble from the people. What makes up this rumble are the rising sounds of people expressing themselves about how they and their families, co-workers, loved ones, friends, and communities are being abused or neglected. That is, they begin forging a sense of solidarity around mutual indignation against injustices that no one should have to tolerate, like the communities in Flint, Michigan, who were ignored too long while being forced to live with filthy tap water that was poisoned with lead. "Of all the concerns raised by the contamination of Flint's water supply," reported Abby Goodnough in the *New York Times* on January 29, 2016, "*and the failure of the state and federal governments to promptly address the crisis after it began nearly two years ago, none is more chilling than the possibility that children in this tattered city may have suffered irreversible damage to their developing brains and nervous systems from exposure to lead . . . Residents and advocates have expressed outrage over the government's failure to protect Flint's children, something many of them say would not have happened if the city were largely white. Adding to their injury, they say, are the harsh conditions of poverty that have already placed ample obstacles in their young lives.*"[58]

A shared sense of injustice, lack of fairness, or oppression is often the first spark in developing a sense of justice about where you want your community and country to go. When the endless daily small talk between people begins to give way to some serious talk about decency and fair play, the "rumble of the people" commences.

In our history that's when the rumble started with enslaved people, Native Americans, farmers, women, laborers, communities of color, and other groups of people who say to one another that life doesn't have to be painful and stifling; it can get better for us and our children.

To my knowledge, no one has figured out a replicable formula to get the rumble underway. It could happen when a person refuses to obey a simple, single humiliating command as did Rosa Parks, or when a community stands up to police violence, as have the people of Ferguson, Baltimore, New York, and dozens of other cities around the country. It could be seasoned organizers rallying workers, like Eugene Debs did, students like Mario Savio, a leader in the free speech movement at Berkeley, or an ethnic group with common grievances like those labor organizer Cesar Chavez and migrant farm workers challenged. It could be a charismatic politician, like fighting Wisconsin Senator Bob La Follette, who took his stimulating rumble to the U.S. Senate. It could be people who start interpreting their daily interactions or observations within a "this is lousy and must be changed" perspective.

A wonderfully insightful and pragmatic organizer in New York City's impoverished neighborhoods, Gabriel Thompson gives us an example of how the *history* of valiant people overcoming injustice can motivate how today you can look at seemingly disconnected instances of injustice with a more sensitive perspective. In his very helpful book, *Calling All Radicals: How Grassroots Organizers Can Help Save Our Democracy*, he writes: "I am not an optimist by nature; I am an optimist by effort . . . It takes effort to see promise in a country where miniature dogs walk down Madison Avenue wearing fleece jackets while families shiver outside soup kitchens. It takes effort to hear empty rhetoric about 'values' from privileged politicians who have never known poverty and then to turn off the television and continue to be confronted with people who must struggle for basic rights like healthcare and housing. And it takes effort not to retreat into the not-quite-happy but safely familiar cynicism and sarcasm that for me is never completely out of arm's reach."[59]

So what helps keep Gabriel Thompson going on overtime confronting the greed of the few over the many, whether in decrepit apartment buildings, poisoned with lead-based paint, or illegal sweatshops? It is the *history* of people "who faced similar situations in the past and whose determination inspires awe. How," exclaims Gabriel Thompson, "could we possibly turn away from them—and what better way to honor the past accomplishments of our heroes than to use them in present struggles?"[60]

The best organizing manuals are books that teach, inspire, provoke, make you laugh and wonder, and cause you to raise your own expectations regarding your significance in making changes you need. Saul Alinsky, the famous neighborhood organizer in Chicago, wrote *Rules for Radicals*. This book can be used today as it was in the 1960s and 1970s by thousands of fed-up Americans around the country. Alinsky was very practical in his tactics and strategies. He once advanced a just cause by threatening the Chicago city aldermen. His tactic was to send his people from the slums of Chicago to fill the toilets at O'Hare Airport, holding up the bladders of thousands of hurrying airline travelers.

One of my all-time favorite "shake 'em up books," which is almost impossible to describe briefly, is Sam Smith's *Great American Political Repair Manual*. As you might expect from a Harvard anthropology major (Class of 1959), Smith fills your gas tank, clears your head, makes you mad laughing, and restores your historical knowledge with excerpts, quotations, and irreverent observations. Smith has an uncanny way of summarizing: to wit, "A few rights a few people have won for you in the Supreme Court since 1932." Or "How Not to Repair the Country: Ten Ways We Really Screw Things Up," or "A 12-Step Program for Recovery from Corporatism," or "24 Cheap and Easy Ways to Make Your Own Media." The book is packed with knowledge about what's happening to us and who's making money and power off the deals. Near the end, he has a few pages titled "How to Find Common Ground" and "How to Do Something About It," with contact information about groups that are fighting the good fight around the country. Tellingly our schools do not use this brilliant manual to teach engrossing practical civics.

On the last page, Smith gives us what is probably his favorite quote by anthropologist Margaret Mead: "Never doubt that a small group of thoughtful, committed people can change the world. Indeed it is the only thing that has."[61]

The book caught the eye of Governor Mario Cuomo, who wrote about Sam: "There are two principal potential objectives in the making of public policy: one is self-interest, the other is the desire to help others. In the plainest language, and with lucid logic, Sam Smith shows us which applies where and, most importantly, he shows us how we can bring the two objectives together to help one another as we help ourselves."[62]

Books like those of Thompson and Smith open up possibilities for ordinary people to perform in extraordinary ways to make life more pleasant, more gratifying, more exciting, less painful, less fearful and less constricted. They also convey a sense of what is possible that grows on you as you read through the pages, and they don't often use words like Republican and Democrats conservative or progressive, red states and blue states, when describing the pathways to the good society. The reason is that they are writing about basic fair play and exposing conditions of deprivation and abuse that can afflict anybody regardless of their position on the political spectrum.

When people break through the abstractions and labels they often find themselves on the same side with their opposites, especially once the discussion gets down to the reality of where people live, work, play, and raise their families. It is precisely because people want the same basic things in life, with obvious variations, that the ruling powers have driven their divide-and-rule strategies throughout history. Such tactics pit people against people over abstract dogmas or ethnicities. This enables self-interested, corporate-sponsored political parties to thrive from such destructive and distractive hostilities.

In the United States the winner-take-all system of elections, the two-party duopoly, and the torrent of funding streaming from plutocrats to politicians who later use the power, resources, policies of governments to enrich their super-donors all serve to deny people real choices and forms of solidarity. Taken together, it is quite a matrix of controlling processes to induce people to line up on one aisle or another while the reins of control are held from on high.

The people of this country must learn to feel comfortable making demands, because by their own recognition, they need—and deserve—so much more for their families and communities. No parents in this country should fear that their child will be shot by the police, but many parents have precisely this fear. No parents should be terrorized by the possibility that their children might be permanently damaged by lead poisoning due to inaction and neglect from their own local government.

Most people have earned far more than they have actually received. You can see the manipulations more clearly when you notice that widely declared divisions among the populace on issues such as reproductive rights, school prayer, and gun rights are immediately highlighted by the commercial media, which can report on such matters with great vigor without it affecting their advertisers. Issues of convergence, solidarity, protest, whistleblowing, alliance building, and early advocacy receive little attention.

In 2000 *BusinessWeek* magazine had a famous cover

feature titled "Too Much Corporate Power?" Inside, the editors devoted several pages with details that answered *yes*! Their conclusion was buttressed by an elaborate poll they conducted asking whether people believed that Big Business has too much control over their lives and that the Big Boys will always get their way in Washington. Seventy-four percent of the responders agreed. One can imagine what the percentage is now following Washington's boomeranging wars of choice and the catastrophic greed of Wall Street that severely battered our country's political economy and the people's livelihoods.

The reason why the plutocrats and their oligarchs have such a serious aversion to any left/right convergence is not just their knowledge that they cannot stop such a powerful unity, but also that underneath such an alliance is the bedrock commonality of what people of the left and right want out of life. They want clean elections and candidates who offer differing agendas. They want their work to be rewarded with adequate returns for the necessities of life, as do "conservative" workers in Walmart. They want healthy food and affordable, safe medicines and healthcare. They want their children to breathe clean air and drink clean water. They want their taxes to be fair and reasonable and well used for the common good in an efficient manner. They want a respected voice in decisions that affect them. They want peace, justice, honesty, and public safety. They don't want the NSA invading their intimate privacy. They don't want their kids to get shot by the police. After some discussion, they'll probably agree with Cicero, the ancient Roman lawyer who defined freedom as "participation in power."[63]

Sure, many Americans feel powerless in the public arena; they can become cynical and withdraw. As Pulitzer Prize winning author Alice Walker has said, "The most common way people give up their power is by thinking they don't have any."[64] If things were otherwise, I wouldn't be writing this small book to advocate that it is easier than people think to turn this country around.

Let's look at some of these areas where a left/right alliance constitutes a big majority. Powered by one percent or less of active citizenry and led by some small full-time citizen advocacy groups, reflecting majority public opinion, we can take back our delegated Congressional power that the plutocrats have hijacked in their favor and return it to "We the People." Here is a short "to-do" list for people across the political spectrum; action on these matters will help us break through power and win greater justice and freedom.

Generate Direct Democracy at the State Level, Revert Airtime to the People to Use on Their Public Airwaves to Debate Issues

There are now 24 states that already have this initiative, referendum, and recall. The same need for direct democracy exists for local government as well. Any time attempts are made to diminish or obstruct direct democracy, conservatives and progressives jointly oppose them. But the people have no media time to counter blizzards of political ads by vested interests. The idea of returning some of the public's airwaves to the public was supported at a House of Representatives hearing in 1991 by me and arch-conservative Phyllis Schlafly. Convergence!

In 1995, when the Republican majority on the Federal Communications Commission (FCC) tried to raise the cap on local media market ownership to 45 percent nationwide and allow any one corporation to own three television stations, eight radio stations, and the leading newspapers in any one local metropolitan market, over 750,000 letters and emails, mostly in protest, were sent to the FCC.[65] They came from progressives and conservatives, from Common Cause to the National Rifle Association. Hard-line conservative *New York Times* columnist William Safire asked, "Why do we have more channels but fewer real choices today?" Mr. Safire's answer: "Because the ownership of our means of communications is shrinking. Moguls glory in amalgamation, but more individuals than they realize resent the loss of local control and community identity."[66]

Defend and Extend Civil Liberties

Most Americans disliked the restrictions in the USA PATRIOT Act as illustrated by agreement between the ACLU and politicians like libertarian-conservative Congressman Ron Paul and progressive Congressman Dennis Kucinich. Both sides also want a more competitive electoral process with easier ballot access, and both question the ineffective mass-incarcerating war on drugs.

Abolish Unconstitutional Acts of War as Have Been Waged Against Korea, Grenada, Vietnam, Iraq, Libya

Enforce Article 1, Section 8, of the U.S. Constitution, which includes the exclusive congressional authority to declare war that U.S. presidents have repeatedly usurped.

Drive Change by Changing Taxation

Increase taxes on pollution, addictive products, corporate crime, and, the big one, Wall Street speculation; and decrease taxation on paid labor and home properties. Remember the motto "tax what we burn before we tax what we earn." Collect uncollected federal income taxes that the IRS estimates to be around 300 billion dollars a year that reflect the ease for many tax escapes by plutocracy: corporations and One Percenters.

Empower People to Challenge Corporations and Government in Court

Allow taxpayers the "standing to sue" the government and corporate contractors. Extreme waste, inefficiency, corruption, and neglect should be just a few of many grounds for taxpayers to hold power accountable in court. Establish rigorous and open procedures for evaluating demands for government bailouts, subsidies, handouts, and giveaways, plus rigorous annual reviews, which would significantly diminish crony capitalism and corporate welfare.

Increase Minimum Wage Nationwide

Increase the minimum wage for 30 million American workers who are making less than workers made in 1968, adjusted for inflation. The inflation-adjusted federal minimum wage would be $11.00 per hour instead of the frozen $7.25 it is today.

Rein in Wall Street

Big banks need to be broken up. Wall Street suits suspected

of crimes need to be investigated, and if prosecuted and convicted, imprisoned like anyone else who commits a serious crime. No more bailouts for big business. Seventy percent of the American people think "most people on Wall Street would be willing to break the law if they believed they could make a lot of money and get away with it."[67]

Audit the U.S. War Machine

Require, at long last, that the Department of Defense budget be auditable and audited by the Government Accountability Office (GAO) of the U.S. Congress. Disclose all government budgets.

Assist Community-level Businesses

Provide an equal playing field for community businesses and community self-reliance and end the unfair advantages that global corporations have lobbied into law.

Crack Down on Corporate Crime, Jail Corporate Criminals

Increase corporate accountability by cracking down on corporate crime, providing updated penalties and enforcement budgets with special attention to corporate crimes involving government programs (Medicare, defense contracting) and against consumers, labor, and the environment. Assert the ownership rights, vis-á-vis management, of individual investors, mutual funds and pension trusts.

Protect the Commons

Charge going market prices for exploiting our public lands,

public airwaves, and taxpayer-funded science and technology presently given away free or at bargain-basement prices. Develop trust funds for people nationwide as the people of Alaska have done with oil-royalty revenues. The Alaska Permanent Fund distributes dividends that in recent years have ranged from a low of $878 in 2012 to a high of $2,072 in 2015 to each human being that has lived in that Republican state for a full calendar year.[68]

Rein in the Fed

Curb the excessive powers exercised by the Federal Reserve through its out of control monetary policies and subject this central bank to Congressional audit and oversight.

All these redirections can be supported by a left/right alliance. They address important areas of reform in our country. They include giving the people effective tools for reforms that are now denied them inside and outside political institutions. Taken together they do reflect Cicero's point that freedom has to be about participation in power. Each of these empowerment proposals should be rolled into one People's Empowerment for Democracy Bill which can serve as a rallying point for one percent or less to get the drive for change underway. Procedural reforms will make it easier to make substantial reforms regarding taxation, illegal war-making, and sovereignty-shredding, so-called free trade agreements.

Therefore, what would activists do to break through power in each of the 435 Congressional Districts? They would agree to volunteer a minimum of 300 hours a year, working together to support and establish offices in each district with at least four full-time advocates to advance their substantive policy agenda. The efforts of these offices and their 4,000 (or less) committed citizens would have two goals. The first goal would be to establish an *in-person* advocacy relationship with their representative and two senators. This is the strategy used by all successful lobbyists. The second goal would be to continually arouse and mobilize the quiet majority of public opinion. The greater the number of people informed, the greater the number of people who will get involved to counter power. Forming local groups to actively spread the word through co-workers, friends, relatives, and larger social networks can have an enormous impact.

No one needs to feel alone. An aura of anticipation, expectations, and overall excitement will arise if all these groups are connected with one another throughout the country. All can learn from one another's stories, ideas, proposals, and strategies. Moreover, in most congressional districts there are almost always some traditional, beleaguered organizations that could be convinced to join ranks and take up the local agenda. Even more, in some districts, there are civic associations, charities, unions, educators who would happily contribute their time, expertise, and donations. These groups are likely to have affiliations with national groups headquartered in Washington D.C. Remember: there are only 535 legislators in Congress and one person in the White House. We are in the millions.

How can we jumpstart this whole process? One way would be to raise money through small contributions and fundraisers to hire staff as quickly as possible. Most people don't personally know any rich people, fewer still know any rich people who are genuinely progressive. If anyone in your local group does, consider forming a delegation to approach them for support. A delegation of twelve people could include educators, parents, clergy, builders, and representatives from local businesses, labor associations, and civic groups. The more varied the delegation, the more impressed your potential donors will be. Your arguments can boil down to a fundamental community appeal for the present and for posterity.

Breaking through power nationwide means designing local campaigns that can spread nationally. Doing so will require a focal point for legislation that will empower people and communities. Here is my suggestion: Call it the Citizens Summons. The Summons will call members of Congress to return home for sustained questioning and education by their voters about the set of points on the citizen empowerment agenda. The advantage of the Citizens Summons umbrella is that it is simple, clear, basic, and personal. It is also new and unusual enough to catch the attention of the media, especially if it gains momentum with a broad base of people across the spectrum of race, income, and political orientation. Politicians are used to running town meetings. The Summons would reverse the process and the dynamic. Henry Thoreau once said that "most people live lives of quiet desperation." We are looking to change our communities into people of rumbling determination.

Accordingly, here is a draft of what a Citizens Summons might look like. It covers some basic derelictions of the Congress, but each local community would shape it and run with it in their own particular way. The main advice is at first to keep it generally centered on the theme of empowerment rather than on a laundry list of reforms that can dissipate your group's initial focus and give your local representative an opportunity to distract you from getting to the more sustainable tools of citizen power.

Empowerment-centered demands could include public financing of elections (preferably through well-promoted, voluntary taxpayer check-offs on tax returns), easier ballot access and voter registration rules, universal voting with write-in and binding "none-of-the-above" options; processes of direct democracy that spell out initiative, referendum, and recall; citizen standing to sue the government, ending corporate personhood and any corporate participation in elections and lobbying (corporate employees could, of course, continue to participate in the electoral process, but not the artificial corporate entity); usable facilities to band together in civic associations as voters, taxpayers, consumers, workers, shareholders, and students; community networks with access to our public airwaves and *control* of the many "commons" that people have legally *owned* for many years so that their use reflects citizen priorities for a prosperous society now and for future generations; and, of course, simple and affordable access to the courts. These empowerments, and others, are spelled out in my proclamation called "The Concord Principles: An Agenda for a New Initiatory Democracy," that I read on a very cold winter day (February 1, 1992), in front of the state government building in Concord, New Hampshire, see: http://nader.org/concord-principles.[69]

An example of the Citizens Summons follows:

The Citizens Summons to a Member of the Congress

Whereas, the Congress has caused gross distortions of our Constitution and laws, our public budgets and our commonwealth, that currently favor the burgeoning corporate state or crony capitalism;

Whereas, the Congress has welcomed the expansion of an electoral system, corrupted by money, that nullifies our votes, restricts our choices, insults our intelligence and commercializes civic values, both Congressional and Presidential elections are so dominated by corporate money that we now have a Congress that is chronically for sale;

Whereas, the Congress has repeatedly supported or opposed legislation at the behest of corporate interests and used many billions of taxpayer dollars to favor the crassest of organized vested interests to the serious detriment of the American people, their necessities, for peace and justice and their public facilities;

Whereas, the Congress has increasingly narrowed or blocked our access to secure prudent behavior from both our government and big business, leaving us unprotected and defenseless in many serious ways, while giving organized, largely commercial interests preferential treatment and allowing them full access to improperly influence or dominate the three branches of government;

Now therefore, the citizens of (insert state for

Senators or the Congressional District for Representatives) hereby respectfully *summon* you to a Town Meeting (preferably during one of the numerous Congressional recesses) at a place of known public convenience. Your constituents will present an overdue agenda of how Congress should shift long overdue power from the few to the many, through the tools we need for the strengthening of responsive, accountable government and vibrant civic institutions. We deem this *Summons*, gaining grassroots support in (your district or state), to be taken with the utmost seriousness as the beginning of a tradition—that will institute a series of meetings expressing the deliberative will of the people. We expect to hear from you expeditiously so that the necessary planning for our Town Meeting can take place. This People's Town Meeting reflects the Preamble to the Constitution that starts with "We the People" embracing the supremacy of the sovereignty of the people over their elected representatives as well as artificial entities, never mentioned in the Constitution, called (global) corporations.

Be advised, that this *Summons* calls for your attendance at a Town Meeting run by, of, and for the People. Please reserve a minimum of two and one-half hours for this serious exercise of deliberative democracy.

Sincerely yours,

(The names of citizens and citizen groups)

Throughout the land, we will see how many signatures are collected and how much time elapses before each member of Congress responds affirmatively. Social media offers a perfect communication tool to drive this "competition."

Professor Richard Parker of Harvard Law School wrote a short book in 1998 with the intriguing title *Here the People Rule*. He asserted that the Constitution provides for an affirmative duty by government "to facilitate the political and civic energies of the people." That is precisely what the tools of democracy and civic engagement enable.

To be concretely helpful, we hope to have a national convocation of citizens addressing the ways and means of making this Citizens Summons a reality in every Congressional District. We expect these proceedings to be streamed, so that you can witness ways you can connect with what is proffered in the following weeks of community energy and action.

There is often a deep and cultivated joy in seeking just outcomes that start overcoming the frequent frustrations and pressures arising out of confronting contentious opponents or stultifying bureaucracies. It is because you are giving expression to what you believe is right, and are helping others, that life is enriched and more significant in the long run. Back in 1993 we asked Anne Witte Garland to interview women who entered controversial civic arenas and challenged powerful interests, from a nuclear plant company to dangerous governmental military policies to an auto company's defective vehicles.

Most of these women had families and had never been activists before. They learned, so to speak, on the job. It wasn't easy. They were subjected to intimidation, ridicule, obstructive tactics, and stresses inside their families. As they dug into their mission, they had to devote more time. After Garland finished her interviews and researched their broader backgrounds, she returned to complete her book titled *Women Activists*. I asked her what was the most memorable impression she took from these women. Her immediate reply: "I have never met happier people."

The combination of joy with justice augments one's fulfillment of life's possibilities. Throughout the centuries, humanity and society have evolved. Progress continues to be made in regard to the rule of law, due process, human rights, and social opportunities. The process has never been smooth and unhindered. War, disruption, and retreat mar every step of the way, but the curve continues upward, notwithstanding the arrival of new risks and uncertainties. Breakthroughs move us forward, but are inevitably followed by new problems that require "thinking anew . . . for a new birth of freedom," to use the words of Abraham Lincoln. The potential for more fair and equable ways to live in one's community, society, and world keeps expanding as well. So do optimistic realizations of what it takes to make changes that somehow escaped our formal education.

Before concluding these shared moments with our kind readers, let's now start together a simple experiment for a long-overdue change in our election laws to provide a role for the disaffected, for the voters who choose *not to vote* for anybody who is on the ballot. It is called a binding none-of-the-above (NOTA) option on every voting line for the disengaged who want to register a "no confidence vote." In our country, when you vote, you can only vote *Yes* to someone on the ballot, unless you write in a vote for someone not on the ballot. This is a cumbersome procedure, to say the least, and in some states and localities, officials don't even bother to count write-ins. I should know.

Only Nevada has a none-of-the-above option, but it is not binding. A binding NOTA option will mean that if there are more votes for none-of-the-above than for any other candidate, that part of the election is canceled and, say in thirty days, new elections with new candidates would begin. Giving ourselves the option to vote for none-of-the-above will bring out more people to the polls. It will shake up smug and stagnant gerrymandered systems where too often just one of the Republican or Democratic Party candidates dominates, or there are two nearly indistinguishable candidates, or no opposing candidate to the incumbent at all. You won't be surprised to learn that, when they hear about NOTA, a majority of the American people favor a none-of-the-above option.[70] Let's get this straightforward movement underway, to exercise a little people power. For a useful manual on how to work for none-of-the-above on local, state, and federal electoral ballot lines, write for a free copy of *NOTA Advance Packet: An Idea Whose Time Has Come* to NOTA, P.O. Box 19367, Washington, D.C. see: http://csrl.org/csrl-books/ and indicate how much time and resources you wish to devote to this initiative and in what electoral district.

Like athletes warming up for a big game, indulging in regular civic calisthenics is good preparation for community capture of Congress. Lone blogger and nudger Alan

DiCara does his bit to keep his Connecticut representatives in Congress sensitive to the anguish of lower-income people, the young people staggering under their high-interest student loan burdens and the costs of health care due to gouging vendors, among other subjects in the news. He talks to and educates congressional staff, writes lengthy, substantive letters to his senators, and lets them know he is watching their performance and sending these messages to his email list. He does this as a citizen hobby on his old computer. Imagine if several million Americans rode herd by themselves on their 535 members of Congress. It would be quite a rumble, even a roar, wouldn't it? It would be a different Congress as well. Can anyone stop you from doing this?

Albert Einstein, who believed that imagination was more significant than knowledge, once said: "Problems cannot be solved at the same level of awareness that created them."[71] Nor are they likely to be solved without genuine spiritual motivation and desire for the common good. Such deeply human impulses must be harnessed to tap our greatest asset over wealth, a weapon against injustice, and tool against a rigged system: love of people and community. By organizing and struggling in this manner, we enrich ourselves and reward ourselves and grow stronger. By organizing and struggling in this manner, we not only fight the good fight, but as we do so, we can achieve the goal of justice, freedom, and democracy: the good life.

ENDNOTES

1. Suzanne Daley, "Speeding in Finland Can Cost a Fortune, if You Already Have One," *New York Times*, April 25, 2015. http://nyti.ms/1HFlg44
2. "62 People Own Same as Half the World," Oxfam press release, January 16, 2016. http://www.oxfam.org.uk/media-centre/press-releases/2016/01/62-people-own-same-as-half-world-says-oxfam-inequality-report-davos-world-economic-forum
3. Catherine Rampell, "Richer Rich, Poorer Poor," *New York Times*, July 10, 2012. http://economix.blogs.nytimes.com/2012/07/10/richer-rich-and-poorer-poor/?partner=rss&emc=rss
4. Howard Zinn, *A Power No Government Can Suppress*, City Lights Books, Open Media Series, 2006, p. 16.
5. Diane Broncaccio, "Nader stops in at Clark's Corvair," *The Recorder* (Greenfield, Massachusetts), November 7, 2014. http://www.recorder.com/home/14260113-95/nader-stops-in-at-clarks-corvair
6. Justin Gillis and John Schwartz, "Exxon Mobil Accused of Misleading Public on Climate Change Risks," *New York Times*, October 30, 2015. http://www.nytimes.com/2015/10/31/science/exxon-mobil-accused-of-misleading-public-on-climate-change-risks.html
7. Justin Gillis and John Schwartz, "Deeper Ties to Corporate Cash for Doubtful Climate Researcher," *New York Times*, February 21, 2015. http://nyti.ms/1Gfgd8l
8. Editorial Board, "A Defense of Sugary Soda That Fizzled for Coke," *New York Times*, December 4, 2015. http://nyti.ms/1YPcwzO
9. Spencer S. Hsu and Victoria St. Martin, "Four guards sentenced in Iraq shootings of 31 unarmed civilians," *Washington Post*, April 13, 2015. http://wpo.st/TpfA1
10. Gary Ruskin, "Spooky Business: Corporate Espionage Against Nonprofit Organizations," Essential Information, November 13, 2013. https://www.corporatepolicy.org/spookybusiness.pdf
11. Nicholas Confessore, Sarah Cohen, and Karen Yourish, "Small Pool of Rich Donors Dominates Election Giving," *New York Times*, August 1, 2015. http://nyti.ms/1Ibs893

12. Tom Wicker, "In the Nation; Improving the Debates," *New York Times*, June 22, 1991. http://nyti.ms/20qyckP
13. Naomi Wolf, "Revealed: how the FBI coordinated the crackdown on Occupy," *The Guardian*, December 29, 2012. http://www.theguardian.com/commentisfree/2012/dec/29/fbi-coordinated-crackdown-occupy
14. "7,000 Occupy Arrests * Return of May Day," Institute for Public Accuracy press release, May 3, 2012. http://www.accuracy.org/?s=Occupy+arrests&submit.x=0&submit.y=0. See also: http://occupyarrests.moonfruit.com
15. Noam Chomsky, *Hopes and Prospects*, Haymarket Books (Chicago), 2010; pp. 31–32.
16. Steven Rendall, "The Fairness Doctrine, How We Lost It and Why We Need It Back," January, 1, 2005, *Fair.org*. http://fair.org/extra-online-articles/the-fairness-doctrine/
17. Jack Ewing, "VW Says Emissions Cheating Was Not a One-Time Error," *New York Times*, December 10, 2015. http://www.nytimes.com/2015/12/11/business/international/vw-emissions-scandal.html
18. *Golden Patents, Empty Pockets*, Mineral Policy Center, Washington, D.C., 1994.
19. Matthew Philips, "Oklahoma Earthquakes Are a National Security Threat; North America's biggest commercial oil storage hub is already on guard against terrorism, but quakes could prove the bigger risk," *Bloomberg*, October 23, 2015. http://www.bloomberg.com/news/articles/2015-10-23/oklahoma-earthquakes-are-a-national-security-threat
20. Benjamin Elgin Matthew Philips, "Big Oil Pressured Scientists Over Fracking Wastewater's Link to Quakes," *Bloomberg*, March 30, 2015. http://www.bloomberg.com/news/articles/2015-03-30/big-oil-pressured-scientists-over-fracking-wastewater-s-link-to-quakes
21. Michael Wines, "Earthquakes in Oklahoma Raise Fears of a Big One," *New York Times*, January 7, 2016. http://www.nytimes.com/2016/01/08/us/earthquakes-in-oklahoma-raise-fears-of-a-big-one.html
22. "Assessment of Admiral Rickover's Recommendations To Improve Defense Procurement," U.S. Government Accountability Office, January 27, 1983. http://gao.gov/products/PLRD-83-37

23. "The FCC, working together with the Consumer Financial Protection Bureau, the Federal Trade Commission, and states' attorneys general has brought a total of $353 million in penalties and restitution against the U.S.'s four largest wireless carriers, structuring these settlements so that $267.5 million of the total will be returned to affected customers." FCC, "Cramming—Unauthorized Charges on Your Phone Bill," https://www.fcc.gov/consumers/guides/cramming-unauthorized-charges-your-phone-bill
24. Matt Taibbi, "Gangster Bankers: Too Big to Jail," *Rolling Stone*, February 14, 2013. http://www.rollingstone.com/politics/news/gangster-bankers-too-big-to-jail-20130214
25. Herman Daly, "War and Peace and the Steady-State Economy," *The Daly News*. http://steadystate.org/war-and-peace-and-the-steady-state-economy/
26. Greg Sargent, "Elizabeth Warren fires back at Obama: Here's what they're really fighting about," *Washington Post*, May 11, 2015. http://wpo.st/37gA
27. "TABLE OF FOREIGN INVESTOR-STATE CASES AND CLAIMS UNDER NAFTA AND OTHER U.S. 'TRADE' DEALS," Public Citizen, June 2015. http://www.citizen.org/documents/investor-state-chart.pdf
28. *Corporate Power in America*, edited by Ralph Nader and Mark Green, Grossman Publishers (New York) 1973.
29. Eric Lipton and Liz Moyer, "Hospitality and Gambling Interests Delay Closing of Billion-Dollar Tax Loophole," *New York Times*, December 20, 2015. http://nyti.ms/1OhyrOw
30. Robert McIntyre, "The Facts About U.S. Corporate Taxes," *Huffington Post*, April 11, 2012. http://www.huffingtonpost.com/robert-mcintyre/corporate-tax-rates_b_1418692.html
31. See CTJ.org for more details. http://www.ctj.org/corporatetaxdodgers/CorporateTaxDodgersReport.pdf
32. Robert S. McIntyre, Matthew Gardiner, Rebecca J. Wilkins, and Richard Phillips, "Corporate Taxpayers & Corporate Tax Dodgers 2008–10" http://www.ctj.org/corporatetaxdodgers/CorporateTaxDodgersReport.pdf
33. Joshua E. Keating, "House of 19,000 Corporations," *Foreign Policy*,

January 24, 2012. http://foreignpolicy.com/2012/01/24/house-of-19000-corporations/

34. "Offshore Shell Games," Citizens for Tax Justice, October 5, 2015. http://ctj.org/ctjreports/2015/10/offshore_shell_games_2015.php#.VxeR0GMsZvM
35. Curtis S. Dubay, "The Bush Tax Cuts Explained: Where Are They Now?" The Heritage Foundation, February 20, 2013. http://www.heritage.org/research/reports/2013/02/bush-tax-cuts-explained-facts-costs-tax-rates-charts
36. Jeanne Sahadi, "Super wealthy: Tax estates more, please," *CNN*, December 11, 2012. http://money.cnn.com/2012/12/11/news/economy/estate-tax/
37. "Estate Tax Statement from Bill Gates, Sr.," December 15, 2009. http://www.faireconomy.org/news/estate_tax_statement_from_bill_gates_sr
38. Transcript of William Gates at Forum on Estate Tax, Urban Institute, January 14, 2003. http://www.taxpolicycenter.org/publications/urlprint.cfm?ID=900584
39. Peter J. Reilly, "Warren Buffett and George Soros Want Higher Estate Tax Than Obama Proposes," *Forbes*, December 11, 2012. http://www.forbes.com/sites/peterjreilly/2012/12/11/warren-buffett-and-george-soros-want-higher-estate-tax-than-obama-proposes/#5007f4601
40. Martin Luther King Jr., Press conference announcing the Poor People's Campaign, December 4, 1967, Atlanta, Georgia. http://mlk-kpp01.stanford.edu/kingweb/publications/papers/unpub/671204-003_Announcing_Poor_Peoples_campaign.htm
41. Alison Gwinn, "Your Pet Explained: The Truth About Cats and Dogs," *Parade*, July 18, 2014. http://parade.com/317088/alisongwinn/your-pet-explained-the-truth-about-cats-and-dogs/
42. "Depraved Indifference Toward Flint," New York Times Editorial Board, *New York Times*, January 22, 2016. http://nyti.ms/1OBpKvG
43. Danny Hakim, "Big Tobacco's Staunch Friend in Washington: U.S. Chamber of Commerce," *New York Times*, October 9, 2015. "http://www.nytimes.com/2015/10/10/business/us-chamber-of-commerces-focus-on-advocacy-a-boon-to-tobacco.html
44. http://www.nytimes.com/2015/10/10/business/us-chamber-of-commerces-focus-on-advocacy-a-boon-to-tobacco.html

45. http://www.pbs.org/wgbh/amex/bomb/filmmore/reference/primary/leebutler.html
46. Tad Daley, "The Nuclear Freeze Campaign: The Largest Political Demonstration in American History," *Public Theology*, February 9, 2011. http://www.pubtheo.com/page.asp?pid=1615
47. "The Reykjavik Summit," The Reagan Vision for a Nuclear-Weapons-Free World, http://www.thereaganvision.org/the-reykjavik-summit-the-story/
48. United Nations Audiovisual Library of International Law: http://legal.un.org/avl/pdf/ha/notewriters/graham_bio.pdf
49. "Overweight and Obesity Statistics," National Institute of Diabetes and Digestive and Kidney Diseases, U.S. Department of Health and Human Services. http://www.niddk.nih.gov/health-information/health-statistics/Pages/overweight-obesity-statistics.aspx
50. Robert D. McFadden, "Everett C. Parker, Who Won Landmark Fight Over Media Race Bias, Dies at 102," *New York Times*, September 18, 2015. http://nyti.ms/1iCqcyJ
51. "CONCEPCION PICCIOTTO, PRESENTE! 1/15/1936–1/25/2016," http://prop1.org/conchita/
52. Caitlin Gibson, "Concepcion Picciotto, who held vigil outside the White House for decades, dies," *Washington Post*, January 25, 2017. http://wpo.st/SXy61
53. "Employee Free Choice Act," LaborUnionReport.com, http://laborunionreport.com/employee-free-choice-act/
54. http://digitalcommons.law.ggu.edu/cgi/viewcontent.cgi?article=1842&context=ggulrev
55. Today, as I write, the residents of Flint can barely get anyone to help rescue them from the poisoned drinking water flowing through their taps. "General Motors even suspended using the water," writes Jesse Jackson, "because it was too corrosive for the auto parts it was making." http://www.detroitnews.com/story/news/politics/2016/01/19/jesse-jackson-flint-wounded-snyder/79036760/
56. Marge Piercy, "The Low Road," *The Moon Is Always Female*, Alfred A. Knopf, 1980. *See:* http://www.pacifict.com/ron/Piercy.html
57. Howard Zinn, *A Power No Government Can Suppress*, City Lights Books (San Francisco), Open Media Series, 2006.

58. Abby Goodnough, "Flint Weighs Scope of Harm to Children Caused by Lead in Water," *New York Times*, January 29, 2016. http://nyti.ms/1OUueO9
59. Gabriel Thompson, *Calling All Radicals: How Grassroots Organizers Can Save Our Democracy*, Nation Books (Boulder, CO), 2007.
60. Ibid.
61. https://www.goodreads.com/author/quotes/61107.Margaret_Mead
62. http://prorev.com/bio.htm
63. http://www.goodreads.com/quotes/106593-freedom-is-participation-in-power
64. http://www.brainyquote.com/quotes/quotes/a/alicewalke385241.html
65. William Safire, "The Great Media Gulp," *The New York Times*, May 22, 2003.
66. http://www.nytimes.com/2003/05/22/opinion/22SAFI.html
67. http://www.thinkadvisor.com/2013/09/24/5-years-on-americans-see-wall-st-as-foreign-a-cul
68. http://www.apfc.org/home/Content/dividend/dividendamounts.cfm
69. The full text is available at https://blog.nader.org/2002/06/06/the-concord-principles-an-agenda-for-a-new-democracy/
70. http://www.field.com/fieldpollonline/subscribers/Release1939.pdf and http://www.nationalreview.com/article/316376/none-above-should-be-ballot-john-fund
71. http://www.alberteinsteinsite.com/quotes/einsteinquotes.html

INDEX

Photograph by Nick Randhawa.

ABOUT RALPH NADER

Named by *The Atlantic* one of the hundred most influential figures in American history, and by *Life* magazine as one of the most influential Americans of the twentieth century, Ralph Nader has helped us drive safer cars, eat healthier food, breathe better air, drink cleaner water, and work in safer environments for five decades.

The iconic champion of consumer rights first made headlines in 1965 with his pioneering bestseller *Unsafe at Any Speed*, a devastating indictment that lambasted the auto industry for producing unsafe vehicles. The book led to congressional hearings and automobile safety laws passed in 1966, including the National Traffic and Motor Vehicle Safety Act.

Nader was instrumental in the creation of the Occupational Safety and Health Administration (OSHA), the Environmental Protection Agency (EPA), the Consumer Product Safety Commission (CSPC), and the National Highway Transportation Safety Administration (NHTSA). Many lives have been saved by Nader's involvement in the recall of millions of unsafe consumer products, including defective motor vehicles, and in the protection of laborers and the environment. By starting dozens of citizen groups, Ralph Nader has created an expectation of corporate and governmental accountability.

Nader's recent books include *Unstoppable*, *Return to Sender*, *The Good Fight*, and the bestseller *The Seventeen Traditions*. Nader writes a syndicated column (see nader.org), has his own radio show (see ralphnaderradiohour.com), and gives lectures and interviews year round.